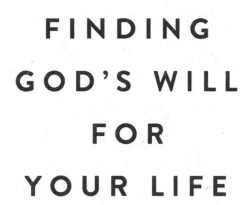

FINDING
GOD'S WILL
FOR
YOUR LIFE

DISCOVERING THE PLANS
GOD HAS FOR YOU

JOYCE MEYER

New York · Nashville

FaithWords
Hachette Book Group
1290 Avenue of the Americas, New York, NY 10104
faithwords.com
twitter.com/faithwords

First Edition: May 2024

FaithWords is a division of Hachette Book Group, Inc. The FaithWords name and logo are registered trademarks of Hachette Book Group, Inc.

The publisher is not responsible for websites (or their content) that are not owned by the publisher.

The Hachette Speakers Bureau provides a wide range of authors for speaking events. To find out more, go to hachettespeakersbureau.com or email HachetteSpeakers@hbgusa.com.

FaithWords books may be purchased in bulk for business, educational, or promotional use. For information, please contact your local bookseller or the Hachette Book Group Special Markets Department at special.markets@hbgusa.com.

Library of Congress Cataloging-in-Publication Data
Names: Meyer, Joyce, 1943- author.
Title: Finding God's will for your life : discovering the plans God has for you / Joyce Meyer.
Description: First edition. | New York : FaithWords, 2024. | Includes bibliographical references.
Identifiers: LCCN 2023050831 | ISBN 9781546005780 (hardcover) | ISBN 9781546007586 (large type) | ISBN 9781546005803 (ebook)
Subjects: LCSH: Christian life. | Spiritual formation. | God—Will.
Classification: LCC BV4501.3 .M4865 2024 | DDC 248.4—dc23/eng/20240108
LC record available at https://lccn.loc.gov/2023050831

ISBNs: 978-1-5460-0578-0 (hardcover), 978-1-5460-0758-6 (large type), 978-1-5460-0580-3 (ebook)

Printed in Canada

MRQ

Printing 1, 2024

FINDING GOD'S WILL FOR YOUR LIFE

Contents

Introduction

Finding God's will for your life is not as difficult as you may think. The first step I would encourage you to take is, instead of trying to "find" it, asking God to show you His will for your life. Instead of focusing solely on trying to hear from God, you can also trust Him to speak to you. We try to do far too many things when we should simply trust God to guide, lead, reveal, and speak to us. When we want to know God's plan for our life, the first thing we need to do is pray, asking God to reveal His will to us. We should pray also for the people we know that they will be filled with the knowledge of God's will for their lives.

In this book, I write about the general will of God for all of us and the specific will of God for each of us. I believe we should first be sure we are doing the general will of God for us as believers in Christ according to His Word. When we are, then God leads us into His specific assignments for us.

God's specific assignments may not seem big, supernatural, or even very spiritual. They are often quite ordinary. But when we do something ordinary for Him and for His glory, it becomes extraordinary.

A man I know was desperately seeking to discover what to do with his life. He was certain he was called to be a missionary, but he was unclear about what part of the world he should go to. India? Africa? Asia? South America? He pondered and prayed about this for so long that he became quite confused. At that point, he sought counseling from a seasoned minister, who listened intently to his concerns and finally said to him, "Do something, lest you do nothing." You see, it is entirely possible that God was not as interested in which part of the world the man went to so long as he went somewhere and began the work he was called to do.

One reason many people find it so difficult to know what God wants them to do is that they don't realize that He leaves many details of our lives to our discretion. When God called me to preach the gospel, He didn't tell me specifically where to go. He simply said to go north, south, east, and west. Since this is a broad statement, I started in my town, St. Louis, Missouri, and organized meetings where I could teach God's Word in the north part of the city, the south part, the east part, and the west part. Some of those meetings took place weekly, and others were scheduled monthly. But I covered all four geographic areas of St. Louis, and the ministry expanded from there as opportunities came along.

As I mentioned, not everyone is called to do something that might be categorized as "spiritual." I say this simply because everything we do is spiritual if we do it for and with God. Even something as simple as the grocery store can become a mission field if we are open to taking every opportunity that crosses our path to represent Christ. Our assignment for a particular day may be to encourage everyone we meet or merely to smile and be friendly. These seemingly ordinary acts are very important to God.

I'm sure you realize that you cannot drive a parked car. As you seek to find God's will for your life, my advice is to get your life out of "park." Start moving in the direction you feel God is leading you. After you take an initial step of faith, you will get more definite direction from God. God told Abraham to go to a place that He would show him, but Abraham had to *go* before anything else could happen (Genesis 12:1).

As you step out in the direction that you believe you are to go in, you can trust that God will interrupt you if you are not going in the direction He wants you to go. Take one step at a time, and if the first step works, take another. If it doesn't, step back and go in another direction. Let me say as I begin this book: Don't be so afraid of missing God that you suffer what I call the "paralysis of analysis." In other words, don't analyze your options for so long that you become stuck and unable to move forward. Overthinking causes a great deal of confusion and can keep you stagnant.

Being led by the Holy Spirit involves learning to listen to your heart instead of your head. Sometimes you simply need to quiet your mind and see what is in your heart—and there you will find God's will.

1

Serve the Lord with Gladness

Serve the Lord with gladness! Come before His presence with singing!
Psalm 100:2

A woman who once worked for us spent a great deal of time seeking God and questioning what His will was for her life, as many people do. One day she came across Psalm 100:2 and immediately knew in her heart that, at least for the present time, God simply wanted her to serve Him with gladness.

Serving God with gladness may not sound like much, but it may be one of the things that God enjoys most. Many of His people are dissatisfied, discontent, and frustrated—none of which reflects His will for us. It is rare to find an individual who can simply be content to do gladly what each day brings. The apostle Paul wrote that he had learned to be content whatever his circumstances might be (Philippians 4:11). Whether he was abased or abounding, meaning "in plenty or in want" (NIV), he learned to be content (Philippians 4:12). When we read Philippians 4:11 in the Amplified Bible, Classic Edition, we see the word *content* explained as being satisfied to the point where we are "not disturbed or disquieted." We can live this way no matter what state we are in. We all want change in certain areas of our lives, but it is important to enjoy where we are on the way to where we are going. This is not only important for our own peace, but when we have this attitude, we also glorify God because it demonstrates our trust in Him. This type of attitude is also a great way to show Christ to other people.

Enjoy where you are on the way to where you are going.

Notice that Paul "learned" to be content. I wonder what had to happen in his life to cause him to learn this important lesson. I imagine he spent some time being discontent and ultimately realized that it did no good. I'm sure he wanted to be happy, as we all do, and we cannot be happy if we are discontent every time our circumstances are less than perfect. Life is full of ups and downs. It is not difficult, nor does it require any faith in God, to be content when circumstances are good, but our faith is tested when they are not good. God uses challenging times to stretch and test our faith, according to 1 Peter 1:6–7:

> [You should] be exceedingly glad on this account, though now for a little while you may be distressed by trials and suffer temptations, so, that [the genuineness] of your faith may be tested, [your faith] which is infinitely more precious than the perishable gold which is tested and purified by fire.

We never know how much faith we have until it is tested. I may listen to sermons on faith and think I know all about it, but when my faith is challenged, I may find I only have mental knowledge about faith and no experience. We learn from God's Word and life's experiences (Proverbs 3:13). The more our faith is tested, the stronger it becomes, until finally we become people who can truly be content in all circumstances because we trust God, no matter what is happening. We have learned from experience that He is good and always does what is best for us.

DO YOU WANT YOUR CHILDREN TO
BE HAPPY?

Dave and I have a four-year-old grandson, and I can tell you that life is much more pleasant when he is laughing than when he is upset or frustrated. Anyone who has children wants them to be happy. It is heartbreaking to see our children depressed, discouraged, and discontent. If you want to know how God feels about you, just think of how you feel about your children. And if you don't have children, think of anyone you love, and you will know what God wants for us, His sons and daughters.

Gladness (joy) is contagious, and we should be contagious Christians. The world is filled with negativity and sadness. When I looked at the news today, I read about 28,000 people who were killed in an earthquake, a woman who was abducted from her home and later found dead, a famous singer who died from a drug overdose, rising prices on almost everything, and shortages of many items we need each day. On and on the bad news went, but the gospel of Jesus Christ is called the Good News, and it certainly is.

We live in the world, but we don't have to let what is happening around us make us unhappy. We can avoid a lot of negativity by simply not listening to or reading too much about all the negative things that are happening. Fill your mind and conversation with all the good things you can think of. Be filled with hope for the future.

Don't let what is happening around you make you unhappy.

You may think, *Well, Joyce, I wish I could be joyful and filled with hope*, and my answer is "You can." Wishing doesn't accomplish much, but action does. Being glad is a decision we make about the perspective (outlook) we have toward life. Some things may not be great, but they could be a lot worse. In many cases, no matter what is happening in your life, there are people going through something worse. I encourage you to think about what you do have, not about what you don't have. Focus on the good things about the people in your life, not just on their weaknesses and flaws. If we would live by Matthew 7:12, which is called the Golden Rule and teaches us to treat others as we want them to treat us, we could serve the Lord with gladness.

The Bible is filled with scriptures about being glad, and without a doubt, being glad is God's will for us. Psalm 126:2–3 says, "Then our mouth was filled with laughter, and our tongue with shouts of joy; then they said among the nations, 'The Lord has done great things for them.' The Lord has done great things for us; we are glad" (ESV).

Multiple scriptures talk about God's face shining on us and making us glad. For example, the writer of Psalm 119:135 says, "Make Your face shine [with pleasure] upon Your servant, and teach me Your statutes." Saying "Make your face shine" is like saying "Smile on me!" Isn't it wonderful to know we can be filled with gladness and that God smiles on us?

TWO WAYS TO JUMP-START GLADNESS

If our car battery is dead, we get someone to put jumper cables on it and jump-start it. In like manner, if our gladness is dead, there are ways we can jump-start it.

There are ways to jump-start your gladness.

Smile

The idea of jump-starting our gladness with a smile may sound overly simplistic, but when we smile, it seems to lift everything up, including our mood. God has given us the ability to smile and laugh, and He must have done this for a reason. After all, His Word says, "A merry heart does good, like medicine" (Proverbs 17:22 NKJV). Sometimes after I have enjoyed a bout of laughter, especially if it lasted very long, I feel as though my entire system has been aired out and energized. In fact, I recall laughing so hard one time that the laughter relieved a headache.

We don't have to wait to smile until we feel like smiling; we can do it on purpose. As the saying goes, "A smile is a frown turned upside down." Start smiling and let it change your feelings. Smile in the mirror every morning, and you will start to see a big difference in your life. Job, in the Old Testament, said he would stop complaining and smile instead: "If I say, 'I will forget my complaint, I will change my expression, and smile'" (Job 9:27 NIV). This is a great example for us to follow.

Make Melody in Your Heart to the Lord

Paul instructs us in Ephesians 5:19 to "Speak out to one another in psalms and hymns and spiritual songs, offering praise with voices [and instruments] and making melody with all your heart to the Lord."

I often find myself unintentionally humming a song that is in my heart, a song I have learned at some time. Recently, I caught myself humming the same tune for almost a week. It was a Christmas song, but it was not Christmastime. I was simply making melody in my heart. This is another way to jump-start your gladness. You can make melody in your heart on purpose, or if you have developed the habit of doing it, you may just find yourself singing or humming without having purposed to do so. I love it when I catch myself humming a tune, because I know it means that joy resides in my spirit.

10 REASONS TO BE GLAD

1. Be glad your name is written in heaven and that you will spend eternity there with the Lord (Luke 10:20).

2. Be glad you never have to be filled with the poison of hatred, because God gives you the grace to forgive those who hurt you (Colossians 3:13).

3. Be glad you can develop and maintain a positive attitude in all things (Ephesians 4:23).

4. Be glad you can be patient. Being impatient only frustrates you and never makes things happen faster (Psalm 37:7).

5. Be glad that God is always with you. You are never alone (Deuteronomy 31:6; Matthew 28:20).

6. Be glad you are loved unconditionally every moment of your life (Romans 8:35–39).

7. Be glad the Helper (the Holy Spirit) lives in you and helps you anytime you need help (Romans 8:11, 26–27).

8. Be glad you have a home, food, clean water, and clothing, because many people in the world don't have these things (Philippians 4:19).

9. Be glad you can help others, because when you do, it will make you happy (Proverbs 11:25).

10. Be glad that God works all things together for your good because you love Him and are called according to His purpose (Romans 8:28).

God gives you the grace to forgive those who hurt you.

I heard a story about a woman who had lost her husband to cancer and her son to an accident within the previous six months. She was so distraught that she thought about killing herself. Day after day, she was depressed and miserable. One day she was walking to the store and noticed a kitten following her. She felt sorry for the lonely, hungry little kitten and took it home to feed it. After she fed the kitten, he rubbed against her leg several times, and she felt the comfort of his soft coat. He purred, and she could tell she had made him happy. Knowing she made him happy put a smile on her face, and then her eyes were opened to the key to being happy for the remainder of her life. All she had to do was stop thinking about what she had lost and start giving what she had left. She started helping others anytime she could and went on to enjoy a happy life.

HOW OUR THOUGHTS AFFECT OUR JOY

Our thoughts affect every area of our life—especially our words, attitudes, and actions. If we think about what we do have and are thankful for it, we will be glad. But if we think about what we don't have and the problems we are facing, we will be sad, angry, and filled with self-pity. We can intentionally redirect our thoughts to the things of God and invite Him to help us. We don't have to think about and meditate on whatever falls into our minds. The Word of God tells us that we can choose thoughts that produce and add to our gladness (Philippians 4:8).

Your thoughts affect every area of your life.

For the weapons of our warfare are not physical [weapons of flesh and blood], but they are mighty before God for the overthrow and destruction of strongholds, [inasmuch as we] refute arguments and theories and reasonings and every proud and lofty thing that sets itself up against the [true] knowledge of God; and we lead every thought and purpose away captive into the obedience of Christ (the Messiah, the Anointed One).

2 Corinthians 10:4–5

This passage tells us that we can cast down wrong thoughts and choose thoughts that reflect God's will. When we learn to think as God thinks, gladness will be our constant companion.

Never forget that God's will for us is to serve Him with gladness.

2

$\approx$

Thank God in Everything

$\approx$

Give thanks in all circumstances; for this is God's
will for you in Christ Jesus.
1 Thessalonians 5:18 NIV

God's will is for us to give thanks in every situation. He wants us to be thankful in all circumstances, because gratitude not only gives praise to Him; it also gives joy to us.

You may be thinking, *How can I possibly be thankful in the situation I am in right now?* I understand that being thankful in a difficult situation doesn't make sense to the natural mind. First Corinthians 2:14 says that the natural (meaning, nonspiritual) person doesn't understand the things of the Spirit. So, if we look at God's instructions to us only with our natural mind, we will often think they make no sense. But the more we grow in spiritual maturity, the more we can discern spiritually what God teaches us to do. When something difficult or tragic is happening to you, you can still give thanks for the good things in your life, and you can thank God that the current situation will ultimately work out for your good (Romans 8:28). Being thankful in all circumstances shows that we trust God to work something positive out of everything that happens to us.

Trust God to work something positive out of
everything that happens to you.

This morning, I was looking through some of my journals from forty years ago, reading about difficulties that were very upsetting to me at that time. Now those situations wouldn't bother me at all, because I have had years of experience with God's faithfulness since then and have watched Him bring good in and from situations that were very painful and unjust when they happened.

You can turn a bad day around quickly if you think of everything you can be thankful for. When we meditate on and talk about nothing but our problems and challenges, life can seem overwhelming, and we begin to murmur and complain. But we have the power to change our attitude anytime we need to do so by intentionally being thankful.

You may not realize this, but complaining is a sin. The Israelites murmured and complained, and

God finally got so tired of it that He sent serpents into the camp, and many of them were bitten and fell dead (Numbers 21:6). Other people were killed due to sexual immorality (Numbers 25:1–9), and still others by the destroying angel, again due to complaining (Numbers 16:41–47). Paul mentions this in 1 Corinthians 10:7–10, stating that these things have been written to warn us not to do as the Israelites did.

If I am sneezing, coughing, and blowing my nose, I have symptoms of allergies or a bad cold. Similarly, if I complain, murmur, and find fault with my life, I am having symptoms of ingratitude. To put it plainly, I am not thankful.

Romans 12:2 teaches us that if we renew our minds according to God's Word, we can discern the will of God because His Word tells us His will. Therefore, the more you know His Word, the more you will know His will for your life.

RELEASE THE POWER OF GOD IN YOUR LIFE

First Thessalonians 5:18 teaches us to be thankful in all circumstances, and verse 19 teaches us not to quench (suppress or subdue) the Holy Spirit. Being thankful releases the power of the Holy Spirit in our life, while complaining quenches it. We need God's power, and we certainly should be careful not to do anything that suppresses it.

Being thankful releases the power of the Holy Spirit in your life.

Sometimes giving thanks is a sacrifice. We may not always *feel* thankful, but we can give thanks anyway, in obedience to God. He appreciates the sacrifices we make because we love Him and want to do His will. It is one thing to be thankful in good times, but it is quite another thing to always give thanks, whether circumstances are good or bad. Psalm 34:1 says, "I will extol the Lord *at all times*; his praise will *always* be on my lips" (NIV, emphasis mine). Thanking God for specific blessings is good, but living with an attitude of gratitude is better. Our petitions often outweigh our praise, and they shouldn't. In Luke 17:11–16, when ten lepers went to Jesus asking for healing, He told them to go show themselves to the priests. As they went, all ten were healed. But only one returned to Jesus to give thanks. In verse 17 Jesus asked, "Were not all ten cleansed? Where are the other nine?" (NIV). This story makes me feel sad because only 10 percent of those healed gave thanks, while 90 percent did not.

After we get what we've asked for, we should not forget God. He warns the Israelites not to do this in Deuteronomy 8:10–11:

> When you have eaten and are full, then you shall bless the Lord your God for all the good land which He has given you. Beware that you do not forget the Lord your God by not keeping His commandments, His precepts, and His statutes which I command you today.

Dave and I do a lot for our children because we love them, and they love us, and the more thankful they are, the more we want to do. I imagine God is the same way. Being thankful for what you have is the quickest way to experience increase.

Being thankful for what you have is the
quickest way to experience increase.

THANKSGIVING AND ANSWERED PRAYER

If we are already complaining about what we have, why should God give us more to complain about? The apostle Paul teaches us to pray *with thanksgiving*:

> Do not fret or have any anxiety about anything, but in every circumstance and in everything, by prayer and petition (definite requests), with thanksgiving, continue to make your wants known to God.
>
> Philippians 4:6

The words *thanks* and *thanksgiving* and *give thanks* appear in the Bible approximately two hundred times, so being thankful is obviously important to God. Are you thankful? Do you frequently voice your thanksgiving to God and to people who help you? The Bible says to be thankful and say so (Psalm 100:4). I believe there are marriages and other relationships that could be saved instead of failing if both parties would simply say thank you more often.

In the Old Testament, Daniel prayed and gave thanks three times a day even after being threatened with harm if he did so (Daniel 6:10). How much different would our lives be if we took time to give thanks three times every day?

THANKSGIVING AND HEALING

I believe that when people have been hurt by one thing, being thankful for other things helps heal their wounds and enables them to go on with their lives. Thanksgiving protects us from the bitterness that often sets in after we have been hurt. Anytime you feel bitterness or resentment creeping into your soul, begin to aggressively thank God for every blessing you can think of. This will protect you from the negativity that will try to fill you on the inside.

Thankfulness also protects us from the poison of jealousy and envy. In addition, thankful people feel less stress than those who are discontent and unhappy most of the time. The less stress we have, the healthier we will be.

Thankful people feel less stress than those who are unhappy.

Whatever we focus on becomes the biggest thing in life to us. Therefore, if we focus on what is wrong and negative, that's all we will see; but if we focus on what is right and good, that's what we'll see. I have observed that positive people often have less illness than negative people do. Once again, we see that negativity puts stress on us, but being positive does not. Even science tells us that happy people are healthier than unhappy ones.[1] Remember, God's Word says that a merry heart does us good like a medicine (Proverbs 17:22).

A THANKFUL HEART IS A GENEROUS HEART

I have found through God's Word and experience that being truly thankful provokes a desire to be generous to others. Here is an inspiring story from the American editor and educator James Baldwin that shows how good character leads to generosity and a desire to help people.

WHY HE CARRIED THE TURKEY

In Richmond, Virginia, one Saturday morning, an old man went into the market to buy something. He was dressed plainly, his coat was worn, and his hat was dingy. On his arm he carried a small basket.

"I wish to get a fowl for tomorrow's dinner," he said.

The market man showed him a fat turkey, plump and white and ready for roasting.

"Ah! that is just what I want," said the old man. "My wife will be delighted with it."

He asked the price and paid for it. The market man wrapped a paper round it and put it in the basket.

Just then a young man stepped up. "I will take one of those turkeys," he said. He was dressed in fine style and carried a small cane.

"Shall I wrap it up for you?" asked the market man.

"Yes, here is your money," answered the young gentleman; "and send it to my house at once."

"I cannot do that," said the market man. "My errand boy is sick to-day, and there is no one else to send. Besides, it is not our custom to deliver goods."

"Then how am I to get it home?" asked the young gentleman.

"I suppose you will have to carry it yourself," said the market man. "It is not heavy."

"Carry it myself! Who do you think I am? Fancy me carrying a turkey along the street!" said the young gentleman; and he began to grow very angry. The old man who had bought the first turkey was standing quite near. He had heard all that was said.

"Excuse me, sir," he said; "but may I ask where you live?"

"I live at Number 39, Blank Street," answered the young gentleman; "and my name is Johnson."

"Well, that is lucky," said the old man, smiling. "I happen to be going that way, and I will carry your turkey, if you will allow me."

"Oh, certainly!" said Mr. Johnson. "Here it is. You may follow me."

When they reached Mr. Johnson's house, the old man politely handed him the turkey and turned to go.

"Here, my friend, what shall I pay you?" said the young gentleman.

"Oh, nothing, sir, nothing," answered the old man. "It was no trouble to me, and you are welcome."

He bowed and went on. Young Mr. Johnson looked after him and wondered. Then he turned and walked briskly back to the market.

"Who is that polite old gentleman who carried my turkey for me?" he asked of the market man.

"That is John Marshall, Chief Justice of the United States. He is one of the greatest men in our country," was the answer.

The young gentleman was surprised and ashamed. "Why did he offer to carry my turkey?" he asked.

"He wished to teach you a lesson," answered the market man.

"What sort of lesson?"

"He wished to teach you that no man should feel himself too fine to carry his own packages."

"Oh, no!" said another man who had seen and heard it all. "Judge Marshall carried the turkey simply because he wished to be kind and obliging. That is his way."[2]

This story describes what I would call a random act of kindness, and I think if we would all practice doing more of these acts, the world would be a much better place. It is obvious that Justice Marshall had a humble and generous heart, and I feel sure he also had a thankful heart, because humility, generosity, and gratitude go together.

GENEROSITY IS GOD'S WILL

Not only does a thankful heart promote generosity, but generosity to others causes them to be thankful to God. Think about these verses:

> For the service that the ministering of this fund renders does not only fully supply what is lacking to the saints (God's people), but it also overflows in many [cries of] thanksgiving to God.
>
> 2 Corinthians 9:12

> God loves...a cheerful...giver [whose heart is in his giving].
>
> 2 Corinthians 9:7

You may be deceived and think you have nothing to be thankful for and nothing to give to others. This is simply not true. If you are breathing, you have a reason to be thankful, and if you can smile, you have something to give that many people need. Some people need an encouraging word much more than they need anything else, and every one of us can encourage others if we will simply take time to do it. By encouraging others, we get our minds off ourselves. The less selfish and self-centered we are, the happier we will be.

If you can smile, you have something to give that people need.

It took me most of a lifetime to realize that giving is a manifestation of love and is the central message of the Bible, but I finally did. Look at John 3:16: "For God so loved the world that *He gave* His only begotten Son, that whoever believes in Him should not perish but have everlasting life" (NKJV, emphasis mine). God loves and He gives. If we follow His example of loving and giving, we will experience His joy. I believe that love is God's will. First, we are to love God with all our hearts, and we are to love others as we love ourselves (Matthew 22:37–40). These are the two most important commandments, and as we obey them, we are in the will of God.

3

~⁓

Offer Yourself as a Living Sacrifice

~⁓

I appeal to you therefore, brethren, and beg of you in view of [all] the mercies of God, to make a decisive dedication of your bodies [presenting all your members and faculties] as a living sacrifice, holy (devoted, consecrated) and well pleasing to God, which is your reasonable (rational, intelligent) service and spiritual worship.

Romans 12:1

Many people frustrate themselves trying to find God's will for their lives, but I don't think we have to do that. Offer yourself to God, as the scripture above directs. When you are available to God, He will let you know at the right time if there is something specific He wants you to do. Until then, live your life as a personal representative of Jesus. He wants to make His appeal to the world through you and me (2 Corinthians 5:20). We are His ambassadors on earth, and this is a great calling even if we never do anything else. People often look for something the world thinks is special—something that will make them feel or appear to be important, but much of that desire is born of insecurity and a need to feel valuable and important. They don't know how special, how valuable, and how important they are to God.

God wants you to find your confidence and security in Him.

God wants us to find our confidence and security in Him, not in what we do. I remember when I worked at my church during my thirties and how thrilled I was when I was assigned a special parking place with my name on it, close to the front door. I also had a seat in the front row of the church with a sign that had my name on it, and Dave had one too. Eventually I was promoted to associate pastor and director of the women's ministry, and I was thrilled to have a title that sounded important. Each week, my name, along with the names of other leaders, was listed in the church bulletin. I felt important seeing my name on that list. I have since learned that while those things were an honor, they were not nearly as important as I thought they were, and they certainly did not increase my importance or value as an individual. God is not impressed with the positions we hold.

I realize now how foolish it was for me to be so excited about seeing my name on a parking place, on a seat, and in the church bulletin, but at the time I was getting my confidence from the wrong places. Eventually God helped me see this and then worked with me to help me place my confidence in Him and Him alone.

What is your confidence in? Is it in what you do or in who you are as God's child? Your *who*, not your *do*, determines your value. If you belong to God through faith in Jesus Christ, you get what Jesus earned and deserves. This is not based on what you do, but on your faith. You and I are joint heirs with Christ through our faith in Him (Romans 8:17).

Fourteen years after his conversion, Paul went to Jerusalem to meet with the apostles. He wanted to present to them his calling from the Lord and the gospel he was preaching to see if they approved, and they did (Galatians 2:1–3). Notice that he waited fourteen years, so he obviously didn't need their approval to be confident enough to follow God's will.

Just as Jesus was not impressed with people's positions and did not play favorites, neither did Paul. He writes in Galatians 2:6:

Moreover, [no new requirements were made] by those who were reputed to be something— though what was their individual position and whether they really were of importance or not makes no difference to me; God is not impressed with the positions that men hold and He is not partial and recognizes no external distinctions—those [I say] who were of repute imposed no new requirements upon me [had nothing to add to my Gospel, and from them I received no new suggestions].

BE AVAILABLE TO DO GOD'S WILL

Henry Blackaby teaches in his book *Experiencing God* that there is a better question to ask than "What is God's will for my life?" The right question to ask is "What is God's will?"[3] Due to our selfish nature, we tend to be concerned only about ourselves, but if we know what God's will is, then we can align our lives with it.

Jesus considered God's will to be His highest priority. He said to His disciples in John 4:34, "My food (nourishment) is to do the will (pleasure) of Him Who sent Me and to accomplish and completely finish His work."

Offer yourself for God's use in whatever way He chooses. Don't be concerned about how important it may or may not appear to others. After offering yourself to God, go on about your life, doing the things I refer to as the general will of God for all of us. If He has some specific assignment for you, He will make it clear to you.

I was making my bed when God called me to teach His Word. I wasn't looking for or expecting to be called into ministry, but I had offered myself to God for His service a few years earlier during a Sunday morning church service. Looking back over my life, I can now see that God was drawing me into the teaching ministry for a long time, but He must work *in* us before He can work *through* us, and that is a process that often takes quite a while.

God must work in *us before He can work* through *us.*

It makes me sad to see people frustrated and striving to figure out God's will for their lives. That is not necessary. Just relax, be ready and willing to do whatever God asks you to do, love God, love people, and enjoy your life (John 10:10).

ALL MEANS ALL

Romans 12:1, which I quoted earlier, says,

> I appeal to you therefore, brethren, and beg of you in view of [all] the mercies of God, to make a decisive dedication of your bodies [presenting all your members and faculties] as a living sacrifice, holy (devoted, consecrated) and well pleasing to God, which is your reasonable (rational, intelligent) service and spiritual worship.

Notice that we are to offer *all* our members and faculties as a living sacrifice to God. This means our mind, will, emotions, abilities, bodies, hands, feet, mouth, eyes, ears, money, time, possessions, and other aspects of who we are.

Are you holding anything back from God? I urge you to make everything available to Him and withhold nothing from Him. In the beginning, this is often a frightening thing to do because we fear that God may ask for something we don't want to give. This is exactly why we offer ourselves as a living *sacrifice*. We may have to sacrifice something, but we will never be asked to sacrifice more than Jesus did. Everything God does or asks us to do is for our benefit. He is not a God who takes, but one who gives. If He does take something, He does so only to replace it with something better.

I love it when people come to me and say, "I want to work for your ministry, and I don't care what I do. I will be happy to do whatever you want and need." These people are extremely valuable. We should offer ourselves to God in the same way. Part of what we call the Lord's Prayer says in Matthew 6:10, "Your will be done on earth as it is in heaven," and this should be our goal.

Jesus didn't want to go to the cross. He asked three times for the cup of suffering to be removed from Him if it was possible, but He always followed His request by saying that He wanted God's will to be done, not His own (Matthew 26:36–44). He wanted God's will more than He wanted His own. Are you ready and willing to do anything God asks you to do? Or do you have something that you want to do, and are you praying that God will bless it? We are always better off when we follow God's plan.

Are you ready to do anything God asks
you to do?

ONE DAY AT A TIME

God rarely gives us the entire blueprint for our lives at once. Instead, He leads us one day at a time. God told Abram to leave his father's house and his country and go to a place that He would show him

(Genesis 12:1). On the day God called Abram, He did not show him where he would end up. But Abram obeyed God's instructions, and God led him day by day from place to place. He lived in tents and had no permanent home, but he believed God, and that counted to him as righteousness (Genesis 15:6).

Following God one day at a time shows that we have faith in Him. You may know God's general will for your life, but the specific plan He has for you each day may only be revealed in His perfect timing. You may go several days or even weeks, months, or years with no instructions at all. When this happens, just keep doing the last thing God told you to do and be willing to serve Him with gladness while you wait.

Keep doing what God has told you to do.

Sometimes we get so caught up doing what we think God wants us to do that we forget to put fellowshipping or spending time with Him first in our lives. Once, when I was working at the church, I was driving to work feeling rather smug that I "worked for God." He whispered in my spirit, "You are proud of yourself because you work for Me, but the problem is that you don't spend any time with Me." I felt convicted in my heart that I had put God first until I got what I wanted, and I then forgot to keep Him first. This is easy to do, but it is wrong. We should always seek God first. When we do this, He will show us more of what His specific will is for us. Over the years, I learned to seek God's face (who He is) and not His hand (what He can do for us). If we seek His face, His hand will always be open. Eternal life is to know Him (John 17:3)—not just to know about Him, but to know Him deeply and intimately. This only happens as we invest time in developing our relationship with Him.

Seek God's face, not His hand.

Don't be surprised if the more spiritually mature you become, the less God speaks to you. In the early years of my walk with God, He seemed to speak to me frequently. But in the past several years, it happens rarely. I believe this is because as we mature, God expects us to know His will and walk in it without any specific instructions to do so. I might say it like this: When I was a baby Christian, God had to shout to get my attention; now He whispers in my spirit, and I can discern His voice. I know in my spirit immediately when I am doing something God doesn't approve of. When that happens, I don't need to pray, I simply need to change direction and align myself with God's will. I am not saying that I do it perfectly all the time, but I am growing, and I have learned to celebrate my successes instead of often being discouraged because of my failures.

GIVING YOURSELF COMPLETELY TO GOD IS A PROCESS

Consider these verses about giving yourself to God. James 4:7 says, "So give yourselves completely to God. Stand against the devil, and the devil will run from you" (NCV). We resist the devil when we submit to God. And Romans 6:13 says, "Do not let any part of your body become an instrument of evil to serve sin. Instead, give yourselves completely to God, for you were dead, but now you have new life. So use your whole body as an instrument to do what is right for the glory of God" (NLT).

These instructions to give ourselves completely to God require dying to self-will. This is not a quick or easy process. Paul writes in Galatians 2:20:

> I have been crucified with Christ [in Him I have shared His crucifixion]; it is no longer I who live, but Christ (the Messiah) lives in me; and the life I now live in the body I live by faith in (by adherence to and reliance on and complete trust in) the Son of God, Who loved me and gave Himself up for me.

While scholars don't agree on the precise date when Paul wrote his letter to the Galatians, we can say that he wrote it approximately twenty years after his conversion, give or take a few years. This indicates to me that it took him some time to reach this point. Remember, he also said that he had *learned* how to be content (Philippians 4:11). Learning takes time and requires going through things and gaining experience with God and His faithfulness.

ENJOY THE JOURNEY

You may be eager to know God's specific will for your life. Does He want you to be in full-time ministry, or should you go to the mission field? Perhaps you should be a nurse or a doctor, a baker or a banker. If you are just not sure, I want to encourage you not to frustrate yourself trying to figure it out. Find something you like to do and do it.

God won't call you to do something that makes you miserable.

God won't call you to do something that makes you miserable. Usually, your natural talents indicate the area of work you are called into. Dave and I know a young girl who is especially gifted in video editing, but she had no desire to go to college or obtain any formal education in that field. Since we have a television ministry, we need people in the audiovisual field, and she applied for a job with our ministry. She then went through the same process of interviews anyone else would go through, and it was determined that she could assist one of the editors, and we would see how she developed. Her talent and work ethic surprised everyone, and before long, she had her own editing suite and was working alone. God gave her talent, and He opened a door for her. He will do the same for you. You may feel led to go to college or you may not; the important thing is to be true to your heart and follow the leading of the Holy Spirit. Good education is wonderful and helpful, but it is not the only thing that qualifies us to be used by God. It is God's anointing (presence and power) that qualifies us.

It is important for you to enjoy your journey through life. Jesus said He came that we might have and enjoy abundant life (John 10:10). Instead of putting the burden of hearing from God on yourself, trust Him to speak to you. When He wants to tell you something, He can make sure you hear Him.

4

~

Learn to Follow Your Heart

~

Trust in the Lord with all your heart and lean not on your own understanding; in all your ways submit to him, and he will make your paths straight.

Proverbs 3:5–6 NIV

God delights in it and considers it beautiful when we are not anxious but peaceful and gentle on the inside, in "the hidden person of the heart" (1 Peter 3:4). The hidden person of the heart is synonymous with the spirit of a person, our inmost being. When we are born again, God gives us a new heart and puts His Spirit in us. According to Ezekiel 36:26, He removes the old heart of stone and gives us one of flesh. To have a heart of flesh means we are sensitive to God's touch; to have a heart of stone means we are resistant to God's will. Often, a hard-hearted person is unmerciful, unforgiving, and harsh in their mannerisms and tone of voice. It is also difficult for them to hear clearly from God. I am thankful that God removes our hard heart and gives us a new heart, making us sensitive to Him. Considering that we have God's heart in us, we are safe in following it because it helps us know His will.

To know what God puts in our heart, we must learn to be quiet and still. Our minds can be filled with many things at once and become quite confused, so as we seek God's will, we need to quiet them and see what is in our heart.

To know what God puts in your heart, you must be quiet and still.

A pastor I know was graduating from Bible college and knew he was called to be a pastor. He wanted to return to his hometown, St. Louis, and start a church. But before he graduated, he was offered a prestigious job at the church associated with the Bible college he attended. He soon became confused and found himself caught between two choices. He needed to make a decision but didn't know what to do. He sought advice from a wise man of God who told him to get alone somewhere, quiet his mind, and see what was in his heart. When he did, he soon realized that going home to start a church was still in his heart; and that's what he did. Had he taken the offer at the church associated with the Bible college, he would have had immediate financial security, while coming home to start a church left him totally dependent on God. I am glad this pastor listened to his heart, because the church he started is where my ministry

began. The path this pastor took was the more challenging of the two before him, but it also brought
much joy and contentment because he knew he was
in the will of God.

GOD LOOKS ON THE HEART

The prayer David prays in Psalm 51:10 is a good one
for us to pray also: "Create in me a pure heart, O
God, and renew a steadfast spirit within me" (NIV).

In 1 Samuel 16, God sends the prophet Samuel
to anoint a new king from among the sons of Jesse to
take the place of King Saul, who had been disobedi-
ent to Him. Samuel looked at seven of Jesse's eight
sons and was tempted to choose the one who had
the best appearance. But God stopped him, telling
him that none of the young men standing before him
was the one. Samuel asked if there were any other
sons, and Jesse said he had a younger son named
David, who was tending sheep in the field during
Samuel's visit. Perhaps due to David's youth, Jesse
had discounted him and didn't even call him in from
the field to be considered as the future king (v. 10).

After Samuel learned about David, they sent for him (v. 11). When Samuel saw him, God revealed to him that David was His choice to replace Saul (v. 12). David had a pure heart toward God.

God often chooses to use people who seem like surprising choices to us. We look at their appearance, their experience, or their past mistakes, but God sees their heart. This was the case with me. To the natural eye, I was not qualified to teach God's Word. I began teaching my first Bible study in short shorts, smoking cigarettes, blowing smoke in everyone's face as I spoke. As one friend said, I didn't have "the right personality" to be a Bible teacher. I was rough, harsh, opinionated, judgmental, and unforgiving, and I had many other characteristics that should have disqualified me. But God saw my heart. He knew I had been sexually abused and hurt very badly, but He also knew that I loved Him deeply and had loved Him since I was a young child. I wanted to serve Him, but I had a lot to learn, and I was willing to learn it. God qualified me by His anointing (grace and empowerment), not my natural talent. And, if He chooses you, He will do the same. He will change you and make you a vessel fit for His use.

We should be careful about forming opinions about people too quickly and take the time to get to know their heart—the real person, who they are on the inside. Too often we judge people without knowing their background or understanding what they have gone through, and we decide they are not useful in God's service. But God knows and understands all things. He looks beyond the way things appear.

God looks beyond the way things appear.

On the other hand, talented people are often promoted too soon, and although they have talent, they don't have pure hearts or motives, and they either cause trouble or end up bringing shame to the cause of Christ. Many of us have heard stories of leaders who have extramarital affairs, are addicted to alcohol or drugs, mismanage ministry finances, and do other disreputable things. Paul even advises not putting a new convert in a leadership position because they could become conceited (1 Timothy 3:6).

God is always looking for people to serve Him, who allow Him to work through them to increase His kingdom. Second Chronicles 16:9 says, "For the eyes of the Lord run to and fro throughout the whole earth to show Himself strong in behalf of those whose hearts are blameless toward Him." He doesn't look for people whose performance is perfect, but instead, God looks for those with a blameless or perfect heart—one that sincerely wants to do what is right and pleasing to Him. You can have a perfect heart and still make mistakes. God can use people with good, pure hearts because they are teachable and will continue to grow spiritually.

GUARD YOUR HEART

Above all else, guard your heart, for everything you do flows from it.
Proverbs 4:23 NIV

We should be careful what we read, listen to, and watch on television. We should guard our heart because it is the storehouse from which we speak and make decisions. Recently, someone was telling me about all the problems at his church. After a while I began to feel irritated. I didn't want to hear that information because I knew it would negatively affect my attitude toward the church, and I didn't want that to happen based on one person's opinion.

The heart is the storehouse from which you speak and make decisions.

When people gossip about other people, it's wise to ask where they got their information. Unless it comes from two or three reliable witnesses, as Scripture says it must (Matthew 18:16), we should change the subject to something positive or be bold enough to tell them we would rather not hear gossip. If we want to walk in God's will for our life, we must guard our heart and keep it pure and clean.

The Bible teaches us to always believe the best of people (1 Corinthians 13:7). This one piece of biblical advice has helped me greatly. Thinking suspiciously and negatively about people is not only *not* God's will, but it makes us unhappy. Good thoughts create happiness, and bad ones create misery. Not all people are good, and at times we must deal with the sinful things they do, but we should pause before jumping to conclusions and seek to discern the truth before forming a judgment.

God speaks to us, or as I like to say *whispers* to us—in our heart. The heart or spirit should be kept in a peaceful or quiet condition, ready to hear and follow God's direction.

SEEK GOD WITH YOUR WHOLE HEART

You will seek me and find me when you seek me with all your heart.
Jeremiah 29:13 NIV

Seek is a strong word. It means to desire, search after, look for, inquire into, examine, consider, strive for, and desire. Jeremiah 29:13 encourages us to make seeking God a priority in our life. We can do this by studying His Word, obeying it, being thankful for all

He does for us, and praying (talking to Him) about everything. We can also seek God by meditating on or thinking about His Word. If you put God first, above all other things, you will soon enjoy a rich, intimate relationship with Him.

When it comes to making decisions, especially major life decisions, it is always wise to seek God first concerning what you should do. You don't have to seek God about every little thing you do, because He has given you wisdom and expects you to use it. However, seeking Him and waiting on Him regarding important decisions provides a safety net for you.

We spend most of our time living from our minds. We think, think, think, and then do what we think. This is not a problem if we think according to God's Word, but if our thoughts are carnal or worldly, then making decisions without consulting God can cause us a lot of trouble. Proverbs 3:6 instructs us to acknowledge God in all our ways. Doing this shows respect for Him. He may frequently approve of what we plan to do, but at least we give Him an opportunity to change our minds if we are going in the wrong direction.

Form the habit of asking God to help you with everything you do. James 4:2 says that we do not have certain things because we don't ask for them, so I think it's always a good idea to ask for God's help in life's major things and in the seemingly minor things. Nothing is too big, and nothing is too little. God is interested in all you do, and He wants to help you in every way you need help.

First Chronicles 16:11 tells us to, "Look to the Lord and his strength; seek his face always" (NIV). God's strength is something I am constantly asking for, and the older I get, the more I ask for it. God can enable us to do anything He wants us to do by giving us His strength.

In Ephesians 3:16, Paul prays for believers to be strengthened in our inmost being. He writes, "May He grant you out of the rich treasury of His glory to be strengthened and reinforced with mighty power in the inner man by the [Holy] Spirit [Himself indwelling your innermost being and personality]." He teaches in Philippians 4:13 (NKJV) that we can do "all things through Christ," because He strengthens us. Don't forfeit God's strength by assuming you can do anything apart from Him. Jesus says in John 15:5 that apart from Him we can do nothing. He wants us to lean on and rely on Him completely.

Hebrews 11:6 gives us a great promise. It says that God is "the rewarder of those who earnestly and diligently seek Him." I get excited when I think of God's rewards. We are not told exactly what they will be, but we can be assured they will be wonderful.

God rewarded Job with twice as much as he had lost after he prayed for his friends who treated him unjustly (Job 42:10). And Isaiah writes that God gives us a twofold recompense (reward) for our former shame (Isaiah 61:7).

God rewarded Job after he prayed for his friends who'd mistreated him.

GOD LIVES IN YOU

Paul says in Colossians 1:27 that Christ in you is the hope of glory, and he calls this a mystery. We cannot understand with the natural mind how God can come to live in our spirit (heart), but we can believe it because God's Word says it. Because He is in us, we should look to our inner being when we are seeking direction. I recall that when I was a baby Christian I often reached out to God and felt I fell short of finding Him. One day I told Him, "I am always seeking You and never finding You." He spoke to my heart, "You are reaching out and you need to reach in." I didn't fully understand what that instruction meant at the time, but over the years I have learned that God whispers in our heart and gives us direction when we need it. God spoke to Elijah in a still small voice, not in loud, thunderous noises (1 Kings 19:11–13).

Not only do we need to learn to develop and maintain inner quiet, but we also need to stop hurrying and rushing so much. We should learn to live in God's rhythm, which is not at a frantic, hurried, noisy pace. It is peaceful and enjoyable. You'll read more on how to hear from God later in this book, but one thing is for sure: We cannot hear from Him if we are not listening, and He will not shout above the noise in our life.

God will not shout above the noise in your life.

Take time each day to wait on God quietly and give Him the opportunity to speak to you if He desires to do so. Go somewhere that is peaceful and be quiet. Let Him know you are listening, and if He doesn't give you any specific direction, then trust that He will guide your steps as you take them. When we seek God's face and seek to live within His will, God will always let us know if we are going in a wrong direction.

God gives us a lot of liberty to make our own decisions. Dave and I have four adult children, and if one of them asks if they can visit us on Saturday, I will say, "yes," unless we have something planned. If we will be home all day, and they ask what time I want them to come, I will probably say, "Whatever's best for you will work for us." God doesn't always have a preference concerning exactly what we do if what we are doing is not in disobedience to His Word.

Think of God's will this way: If you have children and you tell them to go play, you may not have a preference as to whether they play in their room or in the backyard. Similarly, we don't need direction on every minor detail of our lives; we simply need to stay open to changing our direction if God shows us we should.

God gives you liberty to make your own decisions.

5

Take a Step of Faith

For we walk by faith, not by sight.

2 Corinthians 5:7 NKJV

To walk by faith and not by sight means that we live according to what God's Word says, not what we think or feel, and that we believe He speaks to our hearts and guides us. When I sensed in my heart that I was called by God to teach His Word, I saw no evidence in the natural realm that it would become a reality. But I took a step of faith and invited twelve women to a Bible study, and all twelve said yes. My first step worked, so I took a second step and so on. I have taken thousands of steps of faith since that time, but I would not be where I am in ministry today had I not taken that first step.

The first step of faith is often the most difficult to take because we have no experience walking with God in the manner we feel called to walk or in what we feel called to pursue. We are accustomed to living by what we see and feel, so we want to have evidence or see something tangible to let us know we are doing the right thing before we step out. But God works in entirely different ways than what we are accustomed to (Isaiah 55:8–9).

You may wonder what happens if you take a step you believe to be an act of faith and it doesn't work.

The answer is to continue to pray for wisdom and clarity and to continue to trust God's promise that He will guide your steps when you seek His will.

If we are afraid of making a mistake, we will never learn how to hear from God and walk by faith. You never need to be afraid of God—afraid He will be angry with you if you make a mistake, or afraid He won't help you get back on the right path. He loves you and is always willing to help you if you ask Him to.

One time, I truly believed that God wanted me to work at my church. They hired me to be the pastor's secretary, and after one day he came to me and said, "Something isn't right about this. You are not a good fit for this job." Needless to say, I was devastated. But within a short while, he asked if I would teach a weekly women's Bible study at the church. Even though I didn't feel called to teach only women, the Bible study was the only teaching opportunity I had at the time, so I agreed to do it. The first week, 110 ladies showed up, which was amazing because there were only 30 people in the church! The women came from all denominations simply because they had heard about it by word of mouth. They didn't know me, but God drew them to come. The attendance at that Bible study grew to be between 400 and 500 women each week.

Had I remained the pastor's secretary, I would have missed that perfect opportunity. Please remember that the first thing I tried didn't work, but I didn't give up. Walking by faith is a journey we take one step at a time. We step out, and then we find out if what we are doing is God's will for us. If it isn't, there is no reason to be ashamed or feel bad because everyone who walks by faith makes mistakes at times.

If you walk by faith don't be ashamed if you make some mistakes.

When we live by faith, we are like babies learning how to walk. Sometimes we fall, but babies always get back up and try again—and that is all we need to do. The first time I tried to go on television it was an epic failure because I was out of God's timing. Also, the type of program I tried to do was not the type He wanted for me. I tried to host a talk show on which I interviewed various guests. The problem was that when I asked them questions, I usually interrupted their responses and answered the questions myself. In six months of being on the air once a week in my city, we received one or two pieces of mail in response to the program. We assumed that God was not calling us to be on television and we gave it up. Two or three years later, God led Dave to buy a television camera so the teachings I was doing could be captured rather than lost forever. I got a little upset that he bought the camera because he and I had not discussed it, and normally we would have discussed such an expensive purchase.

At that point, we had no idea what we would do with the footage we were recording, but God did. After a short while, once again God spoke to Dave, letting him know that we were to go on television. We had no idea what we were doing or how to go about going on television, but a few months earlier, someone had applied to be a television producer for our ministry, and we simply filed his application. We were not on television, so why would we need a producer? God knew things that we did not know, and He provided the person we needed before we even knew we had a need. God is awesome!

We remembered the producer and called him to come for an interview. He gave us some ideas about how to get started and became our first television producer.

The next step of faith involved money. You can't go on television without money, and we didn't have any money for a project like television. So, we wrote to the people on our mailing list, which was not very large at the time, and told them we believed God wanted us to go on television. We let them know how much money we felt we needed to do it and received exactly that amount of money in response to the letter. You can see how we took one step of faith at a time. To make a very long story short, let me just say that today we are on television in about two-thirds of the world in 110 languages. In March 2023, we celebrated our thirtieth year on the air. What God orders, He pays for, and His will always comes to pass if we step out in faith.

God works through us, not independent from us. But He does not do everything for us either. Walking with God is like a dance. He puts something in our heart, we take a step of faith, and He makes it work. I have seen Him do this for us many, many times. Each time He did, we then took another step, and He made that one work. We are still doing this today. God has been faithful every step of the way, and even though we made a few mistakes, our heart was right, and God always got us on the right track.

ARE YOU READY TO STEP OUT AND FIND OUT?

In Matthew 14:22–33, we read that Jesus' disciples saw Him walking toward their boat on the water of the Sea of Galilee. Peter wanted to walk on water also, so He asked Jesus to invite him to come to Him. Jesus did and Peter stepped out of the boat. He walked on the water for a while and then the wind and waves frightened him, and he began to sink. But Jesus reached out and lifted him up so he wouldn't drown. Peter was the only one of the twelve disciples who walked on water, but he was also the only one who got out of the boat. I'm sure that when Peter stepped out, he wasn't positive he could walk on top of the water. It must have taken courage and a willingness to fail to see if he could succeed. Are you courageous enough to take a chance and risk failure to find out if you can succeed at something you have never done before?

You may be facing new opportunities or new challenges right now. Although in your heart you want to step out, you may be plagued with doubt. If so, I know how you feel, but I encourage you to take the step. Otherwise, you will always wonder what would have happened had you taken it.

Are you courageous enough to risk failure?

According to Colossians 1:4 in the Amplified Bible, Classic Edition, faith is the leaning of our "entire human personality on [God] in absolute trust and confidence in His power, wisdom, and goodness." And Hebrews 11:1 says, "Now faith is the assurance (the confirmation, the title deed) of the things [we] hope for, being the proof of things [we] do not see and the conviction of their reality [faith perceiving as real fact what is not revealed to the senses]."

When we walk by faith, we can fully believe in our heart that something is a reality even though we cannot see or feel it. Because walking by faith is a new way of living, it is often hard to take the first few steps of faith. But eventually living by faith will become natural. God has great things for you to do. Jesus said that we could do the things He did and even greater things (John 14:12). This seems impossible, but with the technology available today, we can reach millions more people in thirty minutes than Jesus reached during His three-year ministry. Of course, we are not the ones doing it; Jesus does it through us. Just remember that He uses people, and He needs each of us to be ready to serve in whatever capacity He needs us. It doesn't matter how big or how small our part is. The important thing is that we step out in faith and do it.

GOD GIVES MANY GIFTS

You probably bought this book because you want to find God's will for your life, as the title suggests. But you may still wonder "What is my part?" Offer yourself to God and He will make it clear to you at the right time.

You may be a helper. Millions of people are. Not everyone stands on a stage or the platform of a church and speaks to people, but those who do need a lot of helpers to get the job done. I know many people who have no desire at all to be the person in charge, but they do want to be involved and help. Helping is a big and vital part of increasing God's kingdom. The more I think about it, the more I realize what a privilege it is to be a helper because the Holy Spirit is our Helper (John 14:26; 15:26). Those who help, share in the ministry of the Holy Spirit. If helping is a good enough ministry for Him, it should be good enough for us too.

---

*Be a helper and share in the ministry of the
Holy Spirit.*

The Holy Spirit is also known as the Comforter
(John 14:26; 15:26). What if God wants you mainly
to encourage and comfort people? Are you willing to
do it? This may sound like a minor role to play, but
once again, if it is good enough for the Holy Spirit,
we should be glad to share in His ministry. Millions
of people need encouragement and comfort, so if that
describes what God has called you to do, you will
never run out of opportunities.

Some people are givers, and they will be gifted by
God to make money. They may own businesses, be
great at investing money, or be inventors. Paul writes
in Romans 12:6–8 (ESV) of seven motivational gifts
God gives to people:

Having gifts that differ according to the grace
given to us, let us use them: if prophecy, in pro-
portion to our faith; if service, in our serving;

the one who teaches, in his teaching; the one
who exhorts, in his exhortation; the one who
contributes, in generosity; the one who leads,
with zeal; the one who does acts of mercy,
with cheerfulness.

He writes of another eight gifts in 1 Corinthians
12:4–11 (ESV):

Now there are varieties of gifts, but the same
Spirit; and there are varieties of service, but the
same Lord; and there are varieties of activities,
but it is the same God who empowers them all
in everyone. To each is given the manifestation
of the Spirit for the common good. For to one
is given through the Spirit the utterance of wisdom, and to another the utterance of knowledge according to the same Spirit, to another
faith by the same Spirit, to another gifts of healing by the one Spirit, to another the working of
miracles, to another prophecy, to another the
ability to distinguish between spirits, to another

various kinds of tongues, to another the inter-pretation of tongues. All these are empowered by one and the same Spirit, who apportions to each one individually as he wills.

We do not get to choose the gift we want to have because the Holy Spirit gives them as He wills for the good and profit of all. In 1 Corinthians 12:28 (ESV), we see another list of gifts, and this one includes administration, which is the gift of organization, without which we would have chaos:

And God has appointed in the church first apostles, second prophets, third teachers, then miracles, then gifts of healing, helping, admin-istrating, and various kinds of tongues.

Paul includes yet another list of gifts in Ephesians 4. Here he notes that included in "Christ's gift" to all believers are apostles, prophets, evangelists, pastors, and teachers, "for the equipping of the saints, for the work of ministry" (vv. 7, 11–12 NKJV).

All your gifts must work together to see God's will accomplished.

As you can see, the gifts God gives to His people are many and varied. The Bible does not state that one is better than the other. To see God's will accomplished, we need all the gifts working together in unity with no jealousy or competition.

I love the following scriptures. They assure us that if we each do our part, God will give the increase and that one of us is not better than the others because of a particular gift. They also tell us that each of us will receive our reward for our work:

> I planted, Apollos watered, but God [all the while] was making it grow and [He] gave the increase. So neither he who plants is anything nor he who waters, but [only] God Who makes it grow and become greater. He who plants and he who waters are equal (one in aim, of the same importance and esteem), yet each

shall receive his own reward (wages), according to his own labor.

1 Corinthians 3:6–8

STAY HUMBLE AND DO YOUR PART

Some people have more than one gift. Sometimes,
they may normally function in a particular gift, but
God may use them in some other gift for a period
of time and for a special purpose. In Acts 6:1–5,
we learn that the apostles of the early church chose
seven men to distribute food to widows so they could
give themselves to prayer and preaching the Word.
One of them was Stephen, who served as a deacon in
the early church, but God also gave him great power
to do miracles among the people (Acts 6:8). In my
opinion, he didn't think waiting on tables and dis-
tributing food was beneath him, so he also had the
privilege of doing miracles.

Remain open for God to use you as He sees fit.

Discovering God's will for our life requires us to remain open for God to use us as He sees fit at any time. We cannot simply decide what we want to do if we want to experience God's will for us. To succeed, we need to seek God's will, step out in faith, believing that the Holy Spirit will guide us according to His will.

6

∽

What If?

∽

*It is better to shoot and miss than to let time run out
and wonder what if.*
Attributed to Michael Jordan[4]

If you do decide to step out in faith, as the previous chapter encourages you to do, one thing you can count on is that your head will be full of what-if questions. Many of them will not be positive, but you can replace each negative one with something optimistic. The ones that try to make you afraid to take steps of faith are certainly not from God; they are from our number one enemy, Satan.

You may have questions such as "What if I fail?" or "What if I try something new and, in the process, lose what I have?" This last what-if is a big one to get past because even though we want to try something new, exciting, and challenging, we don't want to end up with nothing. For this reason, we often settle and stick with what we have rather than risk ending up with nothing. This particular what-if caused me to stay at a ministry where I worked long after God was guiding me to leave and do bigger things. I was afraid that if I was wrong about what I thought He was leading me to do, I would end up not being able to minister to anyone. That fear kept me frozen in place and miserable for about a year. Dave told me I should leave the job and start Joyce Meyer Ministries. Friends told me I should leave. Even a man I didn't know told me he had been praying for me and that God wanted me to stretch out my borders. A woman told me she had a vision that I was root-bound, like a plant that cannot grow because its pot is too small, and that I couldn't grow anymore until I got in a pot of my own, so to speak. I wasn't lacking confirmation; I was just afraid of the what-if.

Thankfully, I finally became so miserable I had to take a leap of faith and follow my heart. I remember my last day at the church where I worked. I walked out of the door with no money, no real direction, and no one to tell me what to do except God. I'm happy to say that He was faithful in guiding me each step of the way. However, at the time I left my job, I had no proof that He would guide and provide. I had to step out into the unknown to find out. It has been a long and not always easy journey, but I am so glad that I confronted the fear and took the shot.

FEAR IS FAITH'S ENEMY

We receive everything God wants us to have through faith, and we lose everything the devil wants us to lose through fear. Fear is the devil's replacement for faith. He perverts the truth of God and turns it into lies, hoping to deceive us. Jesus is truth (John 14:6), and God's Word is truth (John 17:17). The devil is a liar and the father of lies (John 8:44). God is good, and the devil is the evil one. The devil wants us to believe that our past defines us, but the apostle Paul writes that in Christ "old things have passed away" and "all things have become new" (2 Corinthians 5:17 NKJV). The devil tells us that we are alone and that we are the only person who struggles or has as many problems as we do. God promises to be with us always (Matthew 28:20). His Word tells us that believers throughout the world go through the same type of sufferings we face (1 Peter 5:9). Satan tells us we must have the next big thing to be happy, but Paul writes that he learned how to be content whatever situation he was in (Philippians 4:11). The devil tells us it is too hard to forgive, but God tells us to forgive and bless our enemies even as He forgives us (Ephesians 4:32).

You receive everything God wants you to have through faith.

The devil tells us we must be perfect and that being a Christian means we must never sin again, but God is looking for those who have perfect hearts toward Him (2 Chronicles 16:9), even when He knows our behavior is not perfect. Satan's lies are so many that I would not have enough room to list them all in this book. But if we read and study God's Word diligently, we will know the truth, and it will protect us from the enemy's lies.

When Satan says, "What if you fail?" God will whisper in your heart, "What if you succeed?" When Satan says, "What if you end up with nothing," God says, "What if you end up with more than you ever dreamed possible?" Don't just passively listen to the devil's lies; resist them and believe the truth of God's Word instead. If you don't, you will never experience the fulfillment of your destiny because the devil is not only a liar, he is also a thief (John 10:10). Don't let him steal what Jesus died for you to have.

Resist the devil's lies and believe the truth of God's Word.

DON'T BELIEVE YOUR FEELINGS

Emotions (feelings) are quite fickle. They change frequently and without notice. Emotions are some of the believer's most dangerous enemies, and many people are deceived by them. We may feel one way one day and another way the next. Emotions rise and fall, so I advise people to let intense emotions subside before they decide what to do.

If you have integrity, you do what you say you will.

We may commit to something when we are feeling especially good emotionally, but when the emotions wane, we no longer feel like fulfilling our commitment. That doesn't mean we are not responsible for fulfilling it. People with integrity will do what they said they would do even if it is not particularly enjoyable or easy. Psalm 15:4 says that we should swear to our own hurt and change not. This means we should do what we committed to do even if it hurts us to do so.

I learned this lesson in a way that is humorous now, but it was not humorous when it happened. Dave and I were in Florida, ministering at a church. While we were there, we became friendly with a couple on the church staff. One day, I said without thinking about it at all (and that was my first mistake), "You guys should come to St. Louis, where we live, and visit." I went on to say that we could take them to see the sights such as the Arch, the Saint Louis Zoo, and other popular places. I went home and forgot all about the conversation because it never occurred to me that they would ever want to come visit us.

One day the man called and said, "We're ready to come," to which I replied, "Come where?" He said, "To your city—to visit—like you invited us to." Well, I was very busy at the time, and the last thing I wanted to do was to have guests in town. I thought about how I might be able to get out of the commitment, but I knew in my heart that God wanted me to keep my word.

The couple came to St. Louis for almost a week, and we paid for them to stay in a nice hotel per God's instructions. Since Dave was still working in the engineering field, I spent my days taking them sightseeing, and we spent our evenings eating out with them and talking. I learned a good lesson from that experience, which was not to speak unless I think about my words first, especially things like inviting people to do things that would take my time.

My feelings got me in trouble, and I paid a price for following them. Similarly, people buy things emotionally and then regret the purchase when the credit card bill comes. We speak words that cause problems in relationships and then wish we hadn't said them, but there is no way to take them back.

We should be careful about the decisions we make when our emotions are high or low. We may say yes to something in a time of excitement and later regret it, or we might say no to something if we feel discouraged, depressed, or even very tired—and later wish we had said yes.

When emotions are high, Satan will use our emotions to deceive us and make us think we really want to do something we will not want to do when the feeling subsides. Perhaps we ask ourselves too often how we feel about things. This often gets us into trouble we could avoid if we would simply allow our emotions to settle before we make decisions.

Satan will use high emotions to deceive you.

One of the great lessons I have learned in life, and one that has been a huge help to me, is that I don't have to *feel* like doing the right thing to do the right thing. I am to do it despite my emotions. When someone hurts me or treats me unjustly, I rarely feel like forgiving them, but I can do it because it is the right thing to do, according to God's Word (Matthew 18:21–35). If we want to do the right thing, God will always give us the ability to do it. Lean on Him and ask for His help when you are being tempted to do the wrong thing, and ask Him to help you do what is right and godly. Nothing good happens accidentally. It requires a decision to do what is right no matter how we feel or what we think or want. Let's always pray, "God's will be done and not mine."

Forgiving people who hurt us can be extremely difficult, but God has commanded us in His Word to forgive; therefore, we can do it with His help. If we do what God asks us to do, we can trust Him to always bring justice into our lives and situations.

Can you think of times when following your feelings got you into trouble? If so, you can learn from those times and not make the same mistakes in the future.

THE FEELING OF FEAR

Fear is probably the single biggest emotion that prevents people from taking the steps of faith needed to fulfill their destiny. We can feel fear and still not *be* afraid. I have learned that even when I feel fear, I can "do it afraid," whatever "it" is I need to do. We don't have to *feel* bold, courageous, or confident to *be* bold, courageous, and confident. Doing what is right without having feelings to back up our decisions is a sign of spiritual maturity. People who live according to their feelings are spiritually immature and are surely headed in the wrong direction.

You don't have to feel *bold to* be *bold.*

In Joshua 1, God told Joshua that he was the person chosen to finish the job He had given to Moses—to lead the Israelites into the Promised Land (v. 2). He told Joshua not to be afraid because He would be with him (v. 5). Fear basically means to take flight or to run away from. I believe God was telling Joshua that fear would attack him, but that he should not run away, but instead be strong (confident) and of good courage, and He (God) would cause the people to inherit the land He had sworn to give them (v. 6). God repeated His instructions in verse 9, saying, "Have not I commanded you? Be strong, vigorous, and very courageous. Be not afraid, neither be dismayed, for the Lord your God is with you wherever you go."

Joshua had discovered God's will for His life, but he had to confront fear to complete the task God had given him to do. It will be the same with each of us. Once you know what God wants you to do, Satan will try to prevent you from doing it and use fear to accomplish his goal.

After I knew that God wanted me to teach His Word, I needed time to study because I didn't know the Word and was therefore not qualified to teach it. I had three teenagers and a full-time job, so there was no time left to study. I felt God was leading me to quit my job, but I knew if I obeyed Him, we would be short forty dollars for our regular monthly bills each month and have nothing for extra expenses that arose.

I did quit my job, but I remember walking down the hallway of my home during that season of my life and being so fearful that I actually shook physically, and my knees felt as though they would give way beneath me. God whispered in my heart that I could either trust Him for miracles each month or I could worry and be filled with anxiety all the time. I decided right then that trusting God for miracles would be much better. So, for six years we watched God provide in a variety of ways the forty dollars we needed each month, plus the other things we also needed. Those were very hard but precious years. We gained experience with God that has been invaluable to us in the years since that time. I started the journey feeling fear, yet not letting it stop me. I learned that God is faithful.

Nothing is better than personal experience with God. I can tell you that God is faithful and that you don't have to worry, but until you step out into the unknown at His direction and confront the fear that tries to stop you, you will never have the assurance you need to find, do, and fulfill God's will for your life.

7

Can You Really Hear from God?

The sheep that are My own hear and are listening to
My voice; and I know them, and they follow Me.
John 10:27

God is a speaking God. Throughout the Bible there are records of God speaking to His people in various ways. From Genesis to Revelation, depending on the translation, we can read many phrases such as "The Lord said," "God spoke," "The voice of the Lord came to me," and similar words indicating that God spoke to someone. Among others, He spoke to Adam and Eve, Moses, Abraham, David, Isaiah, and Ezekiel. He also spoke to the apostle Paul during his conversion experience on the road to Damascus.

God communicated with His people differently during Old Testament times (before the birth of Christ) than He does in New Testament times (after the birth of Christ), in which we live today. God's people who lived during Old Testament times did not have access to all of God's Word, as you and I do. Because Jesus had not been born while they were living, the New Testament had not been written. Many people, but not all, depending on when they lived, had either some or all of what we call the Old Testament—thirty-nine books divided into the Pentateuch (Genesis, Exodus, Leviticus, Numbers, Deuteronomy; also called the Torah), the historical books

(Joshua, Judges, Ruth, 1–2 Samuel, 1–2 Kings, 1–2 Chronicles, Ezra, Nehemiah, Esther), the wisdom books (Job, Psalms, Proverbs, Ecclesiastes, Song of Songs), and the prophetic books (Isaiah, Jeremiah, Lamentations, Ezekiel, Daniel, Hosea, Joel, Amos, Obadiah, Jonah, Micah, Nahum, Habakkuk, Zephaniah, Haggai, Zechariah, Malachi).

During Old Testament days, the Holy Spirit came on people for special occasions, but He did not live in them as He lives in us today. Instead, it seems that He did speak to people audibly, in dreams and visions, and through the prophets. On one occasion God even spoke to a man named Balaam through a donkey (Numbers 22:21–39). He spoke to Moses out of a burning bush (Exodus 3:1–14); He spoke to the Israelites through a cloud that led them during the day and a fire that followed them by night (Exodus 13:21–22).

We may find ourselves thinking, *To have God show Himself in such visible ways would be awesome!* But the way He speaks to us today is much better because the Holy Spirit lives in believers, and He guides us continually.

Today, God speaks to us mainly through His Word, and He also speaks to our hearts through the Holy Spirit. In addition, He can direct us or send us messages through nature, trusted advisors, circumstances, experience from the past, dreams, visions, prophecy, or a gentle whisper that I call a "knowing" in our spirit about what we should do. He speaks through wisdom, discernment, through peace or lack of peace, and in other ways. He may even speak occasionally in an audible voice, although this is rare. One good guideline to always follow concerning hearing from God is that anything we think we hear or believe is God speaking to us must agree with His Word.

Anything you think God is speaking must agree with His Word.

Before anyone can hear from God on a regular basis, they must believe that God speaks and that they can hear from Him. God desires relationship with His people, and a good relationship is never a monologue; it is a dialogue between two people. I was in church on a regular basis for many years and didn't know that I could hear from God and that doing so was vitally necessary for me. I have since learned that God was speaking to me in various ways at times, as He does to all His children, but I didn't know how to recognize His voice. I wasn't even open to hearing from God because I had never been taught that He would speak to an ordinary person like me. Perhaps you are in the same situation.

If we want to hear from God, we need to truly care what He has to say and be prepared to follow any directions He gives us. We also need to be listening on a regular basis. As I've noted, His voice is usually not like thunder; it is more like a whisper.

God's voice is often not like thunder but more like a whisper.

Most of us are afraid that we will make mistakes as we try to hear God and follow His leading—and we will. Making mistakes is part of learning to hear God's voice. God knows your heart. If you sincerely want to hear from Him and you make a mistake, He will use it to teach you and help you onto the right path. We cannot learn to do anything if we approach it in fear, so I strongly urge you not to start trying to hear from God being afraid that you will make mistakes. If you do, and perhaps you do something based on what you think you heard and then find out you were wrong, don't let that prevent you from continuing to learn in this important area of growth in your relationship with God. If you miss God's direction, He will always find you and get you on the right track again. Don't try to force God to speak to you. Just be assured that if you ask and need to hear something, He will make Himself known. And if you are truly listening, you will not miss His direction.

If you miss God's direction, He will get you on the right track again.

DETERMINING YOUR PATH IN LIFE

Before I write any more about how God speaks to us, I want to make it especially clear that God does not always tell us everything we are to do. Dallas Willard writes in his book *Hearing God,* "In general, it is God's will that we ourselves should have a great part in determining our path through life."[5]

God wants us to live a life of initiative, and He wants us to mature spiritually, just as parents want their children to mature. This cannot happen if someone is always telling us every little thing we are to do. The choices we make reveal the type of person we are, and if we have learned God's Word, we already know a great deal about His will and can make decisions based on that. And because we have His Spirit in us, in general we know what His will is in most situations without needing a specific word from Him to tell us what it is. But for times when we do need a specific direction from God, I can share a few lessons I have learned about how to hear God through His Word and what I have gleaned through my experience with Him.

A great deal of my experience with hearing God is in what I would call general daily fellowship or time spent with Him. I talk to Him throughout the day, and in a variety of ways, and He talks to me. He doesn't speak to me in an audible voice, but through my thoughts, through Scripture, through a magazine, through friends, through a billboard on the side of the highway, and through other simple things that would not be considered super spiritual, but I recognize God saying something through them.

When God is speaking to us, His message always has a little something special that we recognize as being beyond the average or usual way we hear from these sources. We have a sense of certainty or confirmation in our heart that God is speaking. Faith is required to believe it is God speaking to us. But if we don't walk in faith, our other option is fear, and that is not a good one.

GOD SPEAKS THROUGH NATURE

To me, it would be very difficult to sincerely look at nature—animals, galaxies, stars, the moon, the sun, and other creations—and not sense that God is amazing. It seems that it would be impossible to think of how precisely the earth rotates on its axis and to consider all the forests, rivers, and oceans filled with life and not say "There must be a God." Just being in nature can make us feel close to Him. It speaks loudly to me that God is real and active. He calls Himself "I AM" (Exodus 3:14), and He truly is always everywhere we are.

I greatly enjoy watching television shows about animals. I am constantly amazed at the instincts God has placed in them and how He has given each of them a way to protect themselves. Their mating rituals are entertaining to watch, especially a male bird's dance when trying to attract a female. A pride of lions, a family of elephants, a tribe of monkeys, the humorous meerkats, and others all assure me that God is in control. Some animals are so ridiculous looking that I think God surely made them simply to give us a laugh. The sea lion waddling across the beach, the giraffe with its six-foot-long neck, the platypus, and the sloth are good examples.

Consider these Scripture passages:

For that which is known about God is evident
to them and made plain in their inner con-
sciousness, because God [Himself] has shown
it to them. For ever since the creation of the
world His invisible nature and attributes,
that is, His eternal power and divinity, have
been made intelligible and clearly discern-
ible in and through the things that have been
made (His handiworks). So [men] are without excuse [altogether without any defense or
justification].

Romans 1:19–20

The heavens declare the glory of God; and the
firmament shows and proclaims His handi-
work. Day after day pours forth speech, and
night after night shows forth knowledge.
There is no speech nor spoken word [from the
stars]; their voice is not heard. Yet their voice
[in evidence] goes out through all the earth,

their sayings to the end of the world. Of the
heavens has God made a tent for the sun.

Psalm 19:1–4

GOD SPEAKS THROUGH WISDOM AND COMMON SENSE

Many times, considering wisdom and common
sense can help us discern whether God is speaking
to us. For example, if you are praying about whether
to buy a bigger house, wisdom would be to consider
whether you can afford it without it putting yourself under financial pressure. When asking God
if you should say yes to a commitment, ask yourself if adding something else to your schedule will
put you under undue stress. Will it take valuable
time you need to spend with family or getting the
rest you need?

---

*Do not expect God to tell you every move you
need to make.*

Wisdom is what I call "sanctified common sense." As believers, we are instructed to have our mind renewed (Romans 12:2), not to lose our mind and expect God to tell us every move we need to make. Take time to ponder things with God and talk to Him about them before making big decisions—and you will find wisdom whispering in your heart. When making big decisions, take your time and see if you feel the same way after a week as you did initially. Rarely ever do you have to make a decision without having time to hear from God and make sure you have peace about what you should do.

OUT OF YOUR OWN MOUTH

Proverbs 16:1 says, "The plans of the mind and orderly thinking belong to man, but from the Lord comes the [wise] answer of the tongue." I often get the answers or direction I need while discussing a situation with another person. While we are talking, I will say something, and immediately I know that is what I am to do. You might ask, "Joyce, how do you know?" I feel peace about it; it feels comfortable; it fits in my spirit like a puzzle piece I've been looking for. Or, as I said previously, it has that little something extra special that lets me know it is not ordinary, but divine.

God often speaks in a familiar voice. Think about it this way: When your spirit speaks to you, it sounds like you. Of course, we can say to ourselves what we want to hear, so be discerning and make sure you have peace about your decision.

When God called Samuel, he thought Eli was calling him because the voice he heard sounded familiar (1 Samuel 3:1–9). People who listen to me teach a lot have told me things like this: "I started to do such and such, and I heard your voice telling me it would not be wise to do it." In these situations, God used a voice that was familiar to them to speak to them.

DREAMS, VISIONS, AND PROPHECY

God speaks to some people more than He does to others through dreams, visions, and prophecy, and these are areas in which great care needs to be taken. If all my dreams were spiritual, I would have to wonder sometimes if I was even hearing from God. In forty-five years of ministry, I've had only a handful of visions related to ministry and a few dreams in which I knew God was speaking to me. But as I said, God speaks to some people in this way more than He does others.

I am not discounting these as ways in which God speaks, but they are all areas in which it can be easy to be deceived, so I do suggest caution.

If someone shares something with you that they believe is from God, make sure you agree in your spirit that what they are saying is right. For example, if someone prophesies that you are to go to Africa to become a missionary, don't do it unless you know that is what you should do. Perhaps God has already been speaking that to you, and the prophecy is a confirmation.

Do not lead your life according to what others tell you to do.

We should not lead our lives according to what other people tell us to do. If someone prophesies something to you that you don't understand, just put it on a shelf in your mind. A time may come when God will bring it down and use it in your life.

GOD SPEAKS THROUGH YOUR DESIRES

God doesn't speak through the desires of our flesh, but He does speak through the desires of our heart. For example, I may have a desire to give someone something I own or some money, and the desire keeps coming back to me over and over. I have learned to believe a situation such as this is God prompting me to act.

Maybe you find yourself thinking about a certain person for several days. This may be a prompting from God to either pray for that person or just call and say hello. They may need to talk to you but wouldn't be the one to reach out. Or they may simply need the encouragement your phone call would provide for them.

When we delight ourselves in the Lord, He gives us the desires of our heart (Psalm 37:4).

GOD SPEAKS THROUGH YOUR NATURAL GIFTS AND ABILITIES

What does God want you to do with your life? When searching for God's will, especially for your career path, think about what you are good at and what you enjoy doing. Thousands upon thousands of young people graduate high school or college each year and become confused about what to do with their life. Many people have given them advice, but they need to make their own decisions.

Perhaps people have studied in a certain field and can't seem to find a job in that area. I recommend being open to the doors God does open. Although certain opportunities may not seem to be what people want, one open door may lead to another one that is exactly what they desire. The important thing for all of us is to follow our heart and not be afraid to step out in faith.

*When you do what you should be doing, you
will feel fulfilled.*

As I mentioned earlier, I don't believe God will ask us to do something we struggle to do well or something we hate for a prolonged period of time. When we are doing what we should be doing, we feel fulfilled, not miserable. The fact that you *can* do something doesn't mean you *should* do it. I could be an office clerk and do a good job, but that doesn't mean it is what I should do. Many people base their career on how much money they can make, and that can also be a mistake. No matter how much money you make, if you are miserable, it isn't worth it.

It is also good to remember that you may not desire to do the same thing all your life. I did many things before I became a Bible teacher. I was a waitress, a bookkeeper, a credit manager, an office manager, and a babysitter (big mistake). I sold snow cones and worked as a clerk in what was called a dime store—similar to what a dollar store is today. I didn't have a passion for any of those jobs, but each one of them taught me lessons that have helped me in managing Joyce Meyer Ministries.

GOD SPEAKS THROUGH CIRCUMSTANCES

God can open doors and close doors of opportunity in our life. If He closes one, there is no point in trying to push it open. Trying to open it by force will only frustrate you and may even cause serious stress in your life. I firmly believe that what God orders He also provides for, and I can testify that all along the way in our ministry, God has provided the finances and the people we have needed. To me, His provision has been miraculous for more than forty-five years. When we have tried to do something that wasn't God's will or for which it wasn't the right time, it simply didn't work. And after a time of trying to press through the obstacles, we realized we needed to step back and wait for God's perfect timing.

Or maybe someone has been a stay-at-home mom for several years and wants to go back to work, but her children are not old enough to be left alone. If she is conflicted about the right thing to do and cannot find a job or proper childcare, then her circumstance is most likely speaking God's will to her.

God uses circumstances to help you find His will.

God doesn't speak through every circumstance in our life, but He does use circumstances to help us find His will. By watching your circumstances closely, you can sometimes find your way forward.

THE GENTLE WHISPER

God spoke to Elijah through a still small voice (1 Kings 19:11–13). Let me say again: God doesn't usually shout; He whispers. And if you aren't listening, you may miss what He is saying. To hear means to listen and be listening. When I hear God speaking, I have what I call a "knowing." I just know in my spirit what I am to do or not to do. This may be the most frequent way that God speaks to us. Dave and I are trying to decide about something in our life right now, and we don't have that definite knowing, so we are testing the waters, so to speak. We took one step and are waiting to see if that door opens. If it doesn't, we will know to wait. If it does open, then we will take another step, and it won't be long before we will have our answer.

Sometimes I start to do something, and I feel that the Holy Spirit puts the brakes on it. Recently, I wrote a minister a long, encouraging email. I had him on my heart and assumed I was to encourage him, but each time I went to press Send, I just couldn't do it. I sensed the Holy Spirit whispering *Wait*. I had no idea why I should wait, but finally it was so strong that I erased the entire message. It was good that I deleted it, because shortly after that, his drug use, heavy drinking, and improper behavior with women in his church became public knowledge. I had him on my heart, but not for the reason I thought. I'm sure now that God wanted me to pray for the man, rather than write him a letter.

Always listen to the whispers of the Holy Spirit. It will save you a lot of trouble and keep you on the right path as you go through life.

GOD SPEAKS THROUGH PEACE

The Bible teaches us to follow peace (Hebrews 12:14). I refer to this peace as "the inner witness." Paul writes about our spirit bearing witness with the Holy Spirit (Romans 8:16; 9:1). Our conscience is part of our spirit, and it will approve or disapprove of our actions.

This scripture is my favorite when it comes to what God has to say about following peace:

And let the peace (soul harmony which comes) from Christ rule (act as umpire continually) in your hearts [deciding and settling with finality all questions that arise in your minds, in that peaceful state] to which as [members of Christ's] one body you were also called [to live]. And be thankful (appreciative), [giving praise to God always].

Colossians 3:15

The umpire in a ballgame has the final say concerning whether a player is safe or out, and we are to let peace rule like an umpire in our life.

God speaks in small ways, so don't always expect the spectacular. You may occasionally get it, but hearing from God becomes a more normal part of your life if you don't always expect loud, remarkable displays from Him. If you truly want to hear from God, He has ways to make sure that you hear Him, so trust Him to do that.

Don't always expect the spectacular.

Once again, the biggest thing I want to leave you with concerning this subject is to encourage you not to be afraid you will make a mistake. You will make mistakes, and you can make them valuable by learning from them. Have faith that you can and do hear from God, and your faith will open the door for Him to speak.

8

~~~

Doubt and Indecision

~~~

Fear and self-doubt have always been the greatest
enemies of human potential.
Brian Tracy[6]

There are two types of doubt I want us to consider in this chapter: doubting God and doubting self. I think of doubt as fear that is not yet fully grown. And as we have established, fear is the main weapon Satan uses to prevent us from living our God-ordained destiny. God wants us to be bold and confident, not afraid, and He wants us to believe, not to doubt. Believing His promises is the only way to enter His amazing rest (Hebrews 4:3). When we are filled with doubt, we are also filled with confusion, double-mindedness, and indecision.

Indecision is miserable.

I think indecision is miserable. I am a very decisive person and consider myself blessed to be this way. But I know a few people who are very indecisive, and they never accomplish much. Every action begins with a decision, so after making a decision about something, we must follow through with it. Some people have trouble making decisions, and others have trouble following through even after they have decided. They procrastinate, and procrastination is deceptive because it says "I'm going to do it," but somehow it never gets done. Good intentions are not acts of obedience.

Good intentions are not acts of obedience.

Theodore Roosevelt is credited with saying, "In any moment of decision, the best thing you can do is the right thing, the next best thing is the wrong thing, and the worst thing you can do is nothing."[7] Why would it be better to do the wrong thing than to do nothing? Because at least if we do the wrong thing, we learn not to do it again. It deletes at least one option from our choices. Making decisions is extremely important, and we cannot do that if we are filled with doubt.

In *Vine's Expository Dictionary of New Testament Words*, *doubt* is defined as "to be without a way, to be without resources, embarrassed, in doubt, perplexity, at a loss."[8] *Doubt* also implies uncertainty, questioning, hesitation, and not knowing what to do or which way to go. In addition, *doubt* can mean: "to fluctuate in mid-air," or "to keep one in suspense," or "to be greatly perplexed or at a loss." Doubt causes us to waver between hope and fear, and it keeps us anxious and distracted.

Since Jesus is the Way (John 14:6), and He lives in us by His Spirit, we never need to doubt which way to go. Faith in Him and His promises removes despair and crippling doubt. We may not know what He will do, but faith assures us that He will do something at just the right time.

Doubting God's faithfulness comes from inexperience. When we have a few years of experience with God, we learn that He is faithful and always comes through, even if it is at the last minute.

Abraham had every natural reason to doubt God's promise that he and his wife Sarah would have a biological child. When God promised them a natural son, they were both past child-bearing age (Genesis 18:10–11). Becoming parents was impossible, based on the laws of nature. But I love what Scripture says about Abraham in this situation: "No unbelief or distrust made him waver (doubtingly question) concerning the promise of God, but he grew strong and was empowered by faith as he gave praise and glory to God" (Romans 4:20).

SELF-DOUBT

People may believe that God is faithful and not doubt that He will keep His promises, but they doubt that He will come through for them. This is because they don't know their value in Christ, and they don't have a revelation of how much God loves them.

Never doubt that God will come through for you.

When people cannot make decisions, they do not know that they were filled with the wisdom of God from the moment they received Christ as their Savior (1 Corinthians 1:30–31). Wisdom is in us, but we must learn how to discern it and use it. The only way this happens is by acting and finding out what works and what doesn't work. Self-doubt is the fear that we will make the wrong decision.

We learn spiritual lessons the same way a child learns natural lessons. Children learn not to run with their shoelaces untied because if they do, they will get their feet tangled in them and fall. They often must make mistakes and deal with the consequences to learn the right thing to do. Mom may have told them not to run with their shoelaces untied, but they—and we—don't always listen to advice. We resist taking advice for two reasons: self-will and pride. We usually need to learn for ourselves, and often we learn the hard way.

Making decisions is an area in which confidence is very important, so be confident that you have the wisdom to make right decisions. In an attitude of prayer, think about what you should do, and then do what you feel God is leading you to do. Most things will work out well, but occasionally something won't. In that case, simply learn from it and begin again. We cannot find a scripture stating that we will never make mistakes or that God expects us never to make mistakes. The fact that we make mistakes is the very reason Jesus came to be our Savior.

Believe you have the wisdom to make the right decisions.

We all want to be understood, and Jesus understands us. This Scripture passage has encouraged me many times:

> For we do not have a High Priest Who is unable to understand and sympathize and have a shared feeling with our weaknesses and infirmities and liability to the assaults of temptation, but One Who has been tempted in every respect as we are, yet without sinning. Let us then fearlessly and confidently and boldly draw near to the throne of grace (the throne of God's unmerited favor to us sinners), that we may receive mercy [for our failures] and find grace to help in good

time for every need [appropriate help and well-timed help, coming just when we need it].

Hebrews 4:15–16

Even though we have weaknesses, we can still approach God boldly and with confidence (faith) and ask for help, and He will give it.

Believe that God has put good things in you.

Instead of doubting yourself, believe that God has put good things in you and given you the wisdom to make good choices. Philemon 6 says that we are to acknowledge every good thing in us in Christ. We have no problem acknowledging the bad things in us, but God wants us to acknowledge the good things He has put in us because of Jesus. He wants us to believe that He is greater than our weaknesses and that He is working with us to change them. Christ is in us. He gives us wisdom, strength, creativity, righteousness, peace, joy, and all the fruit of the Holy Spirit, to name just a few qualities. And we can always have hope. Peter writes that we are born again into an ever-living hope (1 Peter 1:3). Hope is the expectation that God is going to do something good in our lives, and hope is always available. We truly are filled with good things.

When you believe what God says about you instead of what the devil says about you, your life will change. What you think about yourself is a key factor in determining success or failure. Believe you can hear from God, and believe you make good decisions, because you'll get what you believe when you agree with what God says (Matthew 8:13).

What you think about yourself can determine success or failure.

IGNORE THE VOICE OF DOUBT

Mark 5 tells the story of a synagogue leader named Jairus who went to Jesus, asking Him to come and heal his daughter. As they were on their way to his house, a woman from the crowd touched Jesus. She had been bleeding for twelve years, and as a result she had spent all she had on physicians but was no better. She believed that if she could just touch the hem of Jesus' garment she would be healed. And that's what happened. While Jesus was stopped to talk to her, one of Jairus's servants came and told Jesus not to bother coming because Jairus's daughter had died. The Bible says that Jesus overheard what they said but ignored it. Instead He said, "Don't be afraid; just believe" (v. 36 NIV). He continued to Jairus's house and said, "the little girl is not dead but is sleeping" (v. 39). He took her by the hand and told her to get up, and she did (vv. 41–42).

We don't have to believe everything we hear, especially if it doesn't agree with God's Word or His promises. We may hear it, but we can ignore it. How much grief and emotional pain would it save you if you simply ignored it when you hear that someone has been talking unkindly about you? As I mentioned earlier, I have discovered that believing the best of everyone, as 1 Corinthians 13:7 instructs, is a great benefit to me. When someone hurts me, I can either believe they did it on purpose, or I can believe they didn't realize what they were doing and that their intention was not to hurt me. Believing the best allows me to keep my peace and joy. Even if someone did intend to hurt me, I remain peaceful if I believe the best, and God will deal with them as He sees fit.

Believing the best allows you to keep your peace.

I also ignore a lot of the bad news that is broadcast daily because I believe God will take care of His people. I am not sticking my head in the sand and ignoring reality, but if I hear about something I can't do anything about, why should I let it steal my joy? When the plagues came upon Egypt, God hid His people in a place called Goshen, and the plagues had no effect on them at all (Exodus 8:22). I know our world today is in a terrible mess. Sin is rampant, deception is everywhere, and conditions appear to be getting worse by the day. But I believe that if we as God's children continue to trust and serve Him, He will keep us safe and unharmed. Therefore, I don't waste my time talking and worrying about all the bad news I hear and read daily.

AVOID DOUBTERS AND UNBELIEVERS

When Jesus arrived at Jairus's house to heal his daughter, He didn't allow anyone to go in with Him except Peter, James, John, and the girl's father and mother (Luke 8:51). He wanted to be surrounded by people of faith, not doubters and unbelievers. On other occasions, Jesus had the same desire, such as in Matthew 17:1–25, where we read the account of His transfiguration on the mountain. His face shone like the sun, and His clothes became white as light. Moses and Elijah appeared and talked with Jesus, and once again Peter, James, and John were the ones Jesus allowed to accompany Him. Why? I believe this was for two reasons: He wanted to be surrounded by people of faith, not doubt, and He was training them for their future ministries.

I don't think we fully realize the importance of the people we associate with. We should love everyone and never make anyone feel rejected, but we also need to protect ourselves by choosing godly people to associate with regularly. The people around us affect us greatly.

Fully realize the importance of the people you associate with.

Dave has had a very positive effect on me over the years. He is calm and easygoing. He also has a lot of faith and is extremely optimistic. When we married in 1967, I was extremely negative, frustrated, upset, and worried all the time. I became angry over the smallest thing that didn't go my way. Watching Dave handle situations so differently than I did helped me realize that the ways I had learned to behave during my childhood were not appropriate. Dave was a good example of Christlike behavior, and I became thirsty for what he had. He was salt and light to me, and not only did he make me thirsty for what he had, but his light penetrated my darkness and showed me there was a different and better way to live.

Spend time with the people in your life who are a good influence on you, not those who drag you down and feed your doubt and indecision. After you make what you believe to be a God-inspired decision about something, don't let other people change your mind. People are usually eager to give you their opinion, but that doesn't mean they are right. What they do may be right for them, but not for you. Follow God and follow peace—and you will end up exactly where God wants you to be.

Spend time with people who are a good influence on you.

APPROACH GOD WITHOUT FEAR OR SELF-DOUBT

Ephesians 3:12 says that because of our faith in Christ we can "dare to have the boldness (courage and confidence) of free access (an unreserved approach to God with freedom and without fear)."

Self-doubt is a big problem for people. I believe we doubt ourselves more than we doubt God. For example, when God spoke to Jeremiah and told him that before He formed him in the womb, He had set him apart and appointed him as a prophet to the nations (Jeremiah 1:4–5), Jeremiah's response was one of self-doubt. He gave God a list of his weaknesses but failed to consider God's strength. He said, "I do not know how to speak; I am too young," (Jeremiah 1:6 NIV) to which God replied, "Do not say, 'I am too young.' You must go to everyone I send you to and say whatever I command you" (Jeremiah 1:7 NIV). God told Jeremiah not to be afraid because He was with him and would rescue him (Jeremiah 1:8). He also said, "They will fight against you but will not overcome you, for I am with you and will rescue you" (Jeremiah 1:19 NIV).

Jeremiah obeyed God and went on to become a great prophet. We can feel fear and still do whatever God asks us to do, even if we "do it afraid," as I mentioned earlier.

Moses' behavior was similar to Jeremiah's when God called Him to deliver the Israelites from bondage in Egypt. He offered one excuse after another and mentioned his weaknesses and inabilities in each one. Moses said, "Who am I that I should go to Pharaoh and bring the Israelites out of Egypt?" (Exodus 3:11 NIV). God told Moses that He would be with him (Exodus 3:12), but Moses expressed fear that they would not believe or listen to him (Exodus 4:1). God gave him the ability to perform three miraculous signs to make the Egyptians believe (Exodus 4:2–9), but still Moses doubted himself. His next excuse was that he wasn't an eloquent speaker and was "slow of speech and tongue" (Exodus 4:10 NIV). God told him that his brother Aaron could speak for him (Exodus 4:16). Moses finally ran out of excuses and did obey God.

If God were not with us and for us, we would have ample reason to doubt ourselves, because without Him we can do nothing (John 15:5). But with Him we can do all things (Philippians 4:13).

Decide to believe that you hear from God, that He is with you, and that you are led by the Holy

Spirit. Shakespeare wrote, "Our doubts are traitors and make us lose the good we oft might win by fearing to attempt."[9] The only way to silence the voice of self-doubt is to do what it says you cannot do.

Believe you will hear from God and let the Holy Spirit lead you.

9

Nothing Good Happens Accidentally

Knowledge is not power. It has the potential to be power. It only becomes power when...you apply it and you use it.

Jim Kwik[10]

If you want to find God's will for your life, you must be active and intentional, not inactive and passive. A passive person wants something good to happen, and they intend to sit and wait to see if it does. Active people go after good things. They search, examine, discern, pray, seek, and listen. They walk through the doors God opens, they are not afraid to try things, and ultimately, through this process of following the Holy Spirit's guidance, they will find exactly where they fit into God's plan. But let me remind you again that you don't need to frustrate yourself trying to find God's will for your life, because if He knows your heart is open to serve Him, He will show you at the right time where you fit. Pray about it, leave it in God's hands, and stay active in letting your light shine for Christ while you wait.

You are created for activity, not passivity.

When people do nothing, they become bored and often depressed. We are created for activity, not passivity. Prior to the time God called me to teach His Word, I wanted to serve Him, and I did anything I could do to help the cause of Christ. One summer, I took a group of ladies out once a week, and we distributed ten thousand gospel tracts, placing them on car windshields. I was also diligent about going to church services and studying God's Word because I wanted to learn.

When God is looking for someone to fill a position, He doesn't choose someone who is sitting around doing nothing.

A decision to do nothing is still a choice, one that makes us weaker and weaker. The longer a person does nothing, the more difficult it becomes to do something. In Matthew 25:14–30, we see the parable of the talents (pieces of money). In this parable, before the master of an estate goes on a trip, he gives three men talents according to what they can handle. He gave one of them five talents, one two talents, and one just one talent. Two of the men invested their talents and made more money (vv. 15–17). The third man, who had only one talent, did nothing with his. He simply buried it (v. 18), and when the master returned, he rewarded the two who were active, but the man who did nothing lost even what he had (vv. 20–28). God does not reward passivity.

Do not lose an opportunity by being lazy or refusing to do your part.

In the parable of the ten virgins (Matthew 25:1–13), five of them were passive and lost their opportunity to meet the bridegroom and attend the wedding banquet. Many people lose opportunities because of laziness and an unwillingness to do their part. They prefer to live what they think is a safe life by taking no chances. They may end up safe, so to speak, but they also end up unfulfilled and mired in regret. As I noted earlier, you cannot drive a parked car. If your life is in park right now, it's time to shift gears and start moving in some direction again. If you are moving, God can direct you. But if you are immovable, He will have to pass you by when He is looking for someone to use in His kingdom work.

In Jeremiah 1:12, God says He is "alert and active," watching over His Word to perform it.

Clearly, I believe Scripture teaches us also to be active, not passive. We see this especially in the Book of Proverbs (10:4–5; 12:24; 19:15.) I read an article by a woman who chooses a certain word as a theme for each year, and this year her word is *act*. In the past, she had good thoughts, good words, and good intentions, but never took good action. Fear, passivity, laziness, and procrastination rendered her inactive. Good intentions are good, but they are useless unless we follow them with good actions.

James 2:26 says, "faith without works is dead" (NKJV). We are not blessed in our good intentions, but in actions. And James 2:18 says, "But someone will say, 'You have faith, and I have works.' Show me your faith without your works, and I will show you my faith by my works" (NKJV).

Today's technology gives us access to an abundance of Bible teaching. You can go to church and hear God's Word, watch television and hear it, listen to the radio and hear it, or watch and listen on YouTube, Facebook, podcasts, and more. You can read the Word at home, go to a Bible study group, and memorize Scripture. But none of this does much good if you don't become a doer of what you have heard. Even good intentions don't help us; only acting on what we have learned does any good.

Good intentions alone don't help you.

We learn to truly trust God by applying His Word to our situations and experiencing His faithfulness. When we do this time and again, before long we can trust God in the midst of any kind of difficulty because we know by experience that He always takes care of us. He may not do it in our timing, or in the way we think He should, but He does it, and His plan is always better than ours. I was reminded just this morning when I read Proverbs 16:9 that our minds plan our way, but God directs our steps.

In John 13, we read that Jesus washed His disciples' feet (vv. 3–11). After He finished, He said to them, "Now that I, your Lord and Teacher, have washed your feet, you also should wash one another's feet. I have set you an example that you should do as I have done for you" (vv. 14–15 NIV). He went on to say, "Now that you *know* these things, you will be blessed if you *do* them" (v. 17 NIV, italics mine).

If you know something, you become responsible for doing it.

We may know a lot and still do nothing, and as we can see from Jesus' command in John 13:17, God knows this. I believe that knowledge without action is one of the problems in the church today. I can know I should forgive my enemies and pray for them, but if I don't do it, that knowledge is useless. When we know something, we become responsible for doing it. Paul writes in 1 Timothy 1:12–13 (NIV):

I thank Christ Jesus our Lord, who has given me strength, that he considered me trustworthy, appointing me to his service. Even though

I was once a blasphemer and a persecutor and a violent man, I was shown mercy because I acted in ignorance and unbelief.

I believe Paul received mercy because he believed he was doing the right thing. He was a very religious Jew, and the Jews initially thought Christ and His followers were troublemakers and deceivers. Paul acted out of ignorance, but when he learned differently, he was responsible to act on his new knowledge. James 4:17 says, "So any person who knows what is right to do but does not do it, to him it is sin."

When we don't do what we know we should do, the reason is often that we are deceived through reasoning that is contrary to the truth (James 1:22–24). Let me give you an example of how easy it is to disobey God and not even be aware that you did.

One Thursday morning years ago, I was preparing to teach God's Word at one of my weekly meetings. I was in my closet deciding what to wear and praying for some of the volunteers who helped with the meetings. A woman named Ruth Ann had been a faithful volunteer for a few years, and I asked God what I could do for her. Immediately my eyes fell on a new red dress I had purchased but never worn. It was still in the original plastic bag the store clerk put it in when I bought it.

For a moment, I thought God was telling me to give the dress to Ruth Ann. But my reasoning kicked in, and I decided that couldn't be right because the dress was new. I quickly forgot it and went on to the meeting.

A few weeks later, the same thing happened again. I was choosing something to wear, praying for Ruth Ann, and asking what I could do for her. Once again, my eyes fell directly on the red dress. Although I started to reason again, thinking that it was new and therefore God couldn't possibly be asking me to give it away, I realized I was simply making excuses.

Sometimes giving isn't true giving unless it costs us something. It is easy to give away old clothes we have worn and are finished with, but giving away something new was something I had not done before. I did obey God, and Ruth Ann wore the red dress for several years. She eventually came to work full-time at our ministry, and when I saw her in the dress, I remembered how foolish I had been and how reasoning deceived me to the point of disobeying God without even realizing it.

I told the red dress story so many times as an example of how reasoning can deceive us that before Ruth Ann retired, she gave the dress back to me. I still have it today just to remind me of how dangerous reasoning can be.

Nothing good can happen without action.

God wanted action, not excuses from me. This is what He wants from all of us. When you know God wants you to do something, be sure you do it—because without action nothing good happens.

WATCH AND PRAY

Why is prayer so important? When we pray, we open the door for God to work in our lives or the lives of those we're praying for.

Paul exhorts us in Ephesians 6:18:

Pray at all times (on every occasion, in every
season) in the Spirit, with all [manner of]
prayer and entreaty. To that end keep alert and
watch with strong purpose and perseverance,
interceding in behalf of all the saints (God's
consecrated people).

Other translations render part of this verse: "be
alert and always keep on praying for all the Lord's
people" (NIV) and "being watchful to this end with
all perseverance and supplication for all the saints"
(NKJV). In several places the Bible teaches us to "watch
and pray." For example, we are told to keep watch
concerning the second coming of Christ (Matthew
24:42). We are to watch and pray so we will not enter
into temptation (Matthew 26:41). And we are to "Be
sober-minded; be watchful. Your adversary the devil
prowls around like a roaring lion, seeking someone
to devour (1 Peter 5:8 ESV). These few verses let us
know that a passive person is more apt to get into
trouble than someone who is alert and active.

To watch and pray simply means to be actively watching what is going on around us and pray about it. If we pay attention, we will see many ways we can pray for other people. Anytime you want or need anything, pray about it. Prayer doesn't have to be long and eloquent; just talk to God about whatever you want to talk about, asking Him to help you, provide for you, or guide you. Prayer makes all things possible. One moment of prayer is better than years of worry and reasoning.

A moment of prayer is better than a year of worry.

For example, I had a relationship that seemed to be going sour for no reason I could think of. After four weeks, I realized I had never prayed about it— but I had thought about it, talked about it, been concerned about it, and been confused about it. None of that did any good. But after praying about it, I saw a change in five minutes.

Daily, the enemy tries to steal our faith and cause strife in relationships, and we must be as diligent in prayer as he is in trying to cause trouble. First Peter 4:7–8 says, "The end of all things is near. Therefore, be alert and of sober mind so that you may pray. Above all, love each other deeply, because love covers over a multitude of sins" (NIV).

I often say that love is the highest form of spiritual warfare, and this is because we overcome evil with good (Romans 12:21). We should not allow the devil to distract us from loving other people. Matthew 24:10–12 says that in the last days, "the love of the great body of people will grow cold" (v. 12) because of the wickedness and lawlessness in the land.

We must stay sharp, alert, and active—and not become sleepy Christians who glide along passively, waiting for someone else to do what needs to be done.

What changes would you make if you knew for sure that Jesus was returning next week? If you are smart, you will make them now.

We should be alert for the purpose of prayer, but when we pray, God often shows us something we need to do. And unless we do it, we are just wasting time.

STAY ACTIVE AND STAY OUT OF TROUBLE

Proverbs 16:27 says, "Idle hands are the devil's workshop" (TLB). Truly, idleness, which describes laziness, passivity, or a lack of being active, can lead to trouble. In 1 Timothy 5:11–15, Paul explains why the church should not care for the financial needs of the younger widows. He says that young widows get caught up in their physical desires and lose sight of their faith. If they have nothing to do with themselves, they grow idle, going from house to house, spreading gossip and interfering in other people's business. For this reason, he says, young widows should remarry, so they will keep busy and not fall into sin.

Sometimes when people are experiencing trials and difficulties, they stop going to church or doing the things they normally do to feed their faith. They isolate themselves and sit home worrying and feeling sorry for themselves. This is the worst possible thing they could do. Being idle only opens the door for their situations to get worse. The devil loves to see a person be inactive and idle, because it is easier for him to tempt someone in that condition to do wrong things than it is for him to tempt someone who is focused and busy. But when we stay active, learning and doing what God's Word says, praying, and helping other people, we put ourselves in a safe place while God is solving our problems. Any time you are having problems, you need more of God and of spiritual things, not less.

A woman I knew lost her daughter to cancer. The very next week, she was back at church and had gone through her closet and taken out several items to give to people. I was amazed and proud of her because she was fighting the devil with good, which is the way we overcome evil (Romans 12:21).

Although our enemy, the devil, is looking for someone to devour, we can protect ourselves by being firm in faith and continuing to stay alert and active in obedience to God just as 1 Peter 5:8–9 says:

Be well balanced (temperate, sober of mind), be vigilant and cautious at all times; for that enemy of yours, the devil, roams around like a lion roaring [in fierce hunger], seeking someone to seize upon and devour. Withstand him; be firm in faith [against his onset—rooted, established, strong, immovable, and determined].

10

Follow Peace and
Enjoy Life

*May the God of your hope so fill you with all joy
and peace in believing [through the experience of
your faith] that by the power of the Holy Spirit you
may abound and be overflowing (bubbling over)
with hope.*

Romans 15:13

P eace and joy are two of the most important qualities we need to enjoy our life. If we are upset
and sad most of the time, we will not enjoy anything,
no matter what else we have. In Romans 14:17, Paul
writes, "The kingdom of God is not a matter of eating and drinking, but of righteousness, peace and joy
in the Holy Spirit" (NIV). To put this verse in context,
the Jewish people had many rules about eating and
drinking, and Paul was trying to teach them that Jesus
had set them free from these rules. He wanted them
to concentrate on righteousness (being and doing
right), peace, and joy. I like to say that the kingdom
of God is not about things but about righteousness,
peace, and joy. We can only have these qualities as we
believe God's Word and put our faith in Him.

Christianity doesn't begin with a do *but
with a* done.

To explain what I mean when I say "being right,"
let me say that our righteousness (being right with

God) as believers in Christ is found in our faith in Jesus. Our "right" deeds don't make us right with God; our faith in Jesus does. We must *be made* right before we can *do* right. Christianity doesn't begin with a *do* but with a *done*. It is all about what Jesus has done, not what we can do. Second Corinthians 5:21 says:

> For our sake He made Christ [virtually] to be sin Who knew no sin, so that in and through Him we might become [endued with, viewed as being in, and examples of] the righteousness of God [what we ought to be, approved and acceptable and in right relationship with Him, by His goodness].

Peace and joy are God's will for your life. Even if you discover something specific you believe you are destined to do, if you don't have peace and joy, you'll miss God's best for you. As I mentioned earlier in this book, it is important that we fulfill the general will of God for our life before searching for what He specifically wants us to do.

PEACE

Peace is the opposite of anxiety, upset, distress, worry, and distressing care. We waste a great deal of time sacrificing our peace by worrying, and this does no good at all. Worry has never solved a problem for anyone, but it does create stress and deplete us of energy.

Paul teaches that we should let peace be the umpire in our life in regard to hearing from God. In other words, peace should be the deciding factor regarding whether or not we do something or allow something in our lives. If we have peace, it is a green light (meaning to go ahead and do or allow something), and if we don't have peace, it is a red light (meaning to stop). I mentioned this verse earlier but would like us to look at it again. It reads:

And let the peace (soul harmony which comes) from Christ rule (act as umpire continually) in your hearts [deciding and settling with finality all questions that arise in your minds, in that peaceful state] to which as [members of Christ's] one body you were also called [to

live]. And be thankful (appreciative), [giving
praise to God always].

Colossians 3:15

When emotions are running high, we can feel a
false sense of peace. Here's an example to explain what
I mean. A few years ago, I had the idea to build a new
house next door to my daughter. She wanted Dave
and me to do this, and so did I. She does a lot to help
us, and we reasoned that things would be so much
easier if we lived right next door to her. We are only
three minutes away from her as it is, but if we were
next door, she wouldn't have to drive to our house; she
could just walk over. We went so far as to start having
plans drawn for the new house. But interestingly, once
my emotions settled down, I started realizing I did not
have peace about building a house; I didn't even want
to do it. Emotions can be very deceptive, and we need
to be careful about making decisions when our feelings are running high and we are excited. I felt foolish, but I had to go back to everyone I had enlisted to
help with my scheme and tell them I didn't hear from
God—that I had made an emotional decision and had

no peace about moving. We may someday build a house next to hers, but when I had the idea and began to put my plan in motion, the timing wasn't right.

After having this type of experience on more than one occasion, I have learned to wait before I announce my big ideas, and I've learned to give God time to whisper in my spirit what His will is. I am especially diligent about this if the decision is a big one.

Before Jesus ascended to heaven, He told His disciples that He would leave them His peace (John 14:27). To receive His peace, we must stop allowing ourselves to get upset. You may think you can't help it if you get upset, but that is not true. As believers, we have self-control as a fruit of the Holy Spirit (Galatians 5:22–23), and the best way to deal with anxiety and being upset is to stop these feelings when they start. First Peter 5:8–9 teaches us to resist the devil "against his onset," and I have found this to be great advice. Talk to yourself. Remind yourself that getting upset won't change a situation, but it may lead you to do something you will later regret.

When anxiety attacks, our first response should be to pray. And instead of worrying, we should thank

God for the many wonderful things He has done for us. When we do this, the peace of God will guard our hearts and minds (Philippians 4:6–7).

Walt Whitman said, "Peace is always beautiful,"[11] and he is correct. A peaceful life is indeed a beautiful life. Roy Bennett said, "Learning to distance yourself from all the negativity is one of the greatest lessons to achieve inner peace."[12]

Living in peace is a decision.

Living in peace is a decision, and it usually requires some changes in the way we do certain things. Jesus is the perfect picture of peace. We can learn from studying His life that:

- He was never in a hurry.
- He took time to pray.
- He didn't get upset when people said bad things about Him because He knew His own heart.

- He forgave those who hurt Him and taught us to forgive.
- He didn't worry, and He was peaceful even in the storms of life.

Peace was a priority for Jesus, and it must be for us also.

First Peter 3:11 says that we "must seek peace and pursue it" (NIV). This one scripture has been life-changing for me because it helped me to realize I couldn't simply wish for peace or pray for peace; I had to pursue it. I realized I had to change my approach to many things if I truly wanted to have peace.

As I searched for and pursued peace, I also found that I needed a lot more humility than I currently had. Why humility? I found that trying to prove I was right in a conflict always resulted in a loss of peace, so I learned to humble myself and choose peace over being right about my opinions. Being right in a disagreement is highly overrated anyway. Of course, there are times we need to stand our ground about something we believe in, but fighting about it is never the solution. I learned to agree to disagree and to respect other people's opinions even when they didn't agree with me. Not giving my opinion so often took humility, and I found that minding my own business is a pathway to peace for me. One of the big lessons I had to learn was when to just be quiet and not feel I needed to have the last word in a disagreement, especially between family members.

Respect the opinions of others even when they don't agree with yours.

I don't always do things right, but I have come a long way, and I enjoy much more peace than I used to. I grew up in a dysfunctional household that was full of strife, and peace was not something I knew much about. I had a lot to learn, but I eventually did learn that we can hold our peace if we sincerely want to.

God told the Israelites when they were in battle that He would fight for them and that they were to hold their peace and remain at rest (Exodus 14:14).

Being at peace is a pleasant way to win the war with the devil. Ephesians 6:12–13 says:

For we are not wrestling with flesh and blood [contending only with physical opponents], but against the despotisms, against the powers, against [the master spirits who are] the world rulers of this present darkness, against the spirit forces of wickedness in the heavenly (supernatural) sphere. Therefore, put on God's complete armor, that you may be able to resist and stand your ground on the evil day [of danger], and, having done all [the crisis demands], to stand [firmly in your place].

Our spiritual armor listed in Ephesians 6:14–17 includes what I call our "shoes of peace" (v. 15), and wearing those shoes, spiritually speaking, means walking through life in peace. When the devil is trying to upset you, and you hold your peace, he loses the battle. When Paul was encouraging the church in Rome, he told them that "the God of peace will soon crush Satan under your feet" (Romans 16:20).

I read that the word *peace* appears 329 times in the Bible, and thirty of them are in the book of Isaiah.[13] I am sure this number varies by Bible translation, but I want to make the point that peace is God's will for our life. It is obviously very important if it is mentioned so many times in God's Word.

ENJOYING LIFE

Jesus says that the devil comes to steal, kill, and destroy, but that He came so we could have life and enjoy our lives to the fullest (John 10:10). I wrote in chapter 1 about serving the Lord with gladness, but this principle is so important that I feel it's a good idea to present it from a little different angle in this chapter.

We read earlier that peace and joy come from believing, so if you have lost your joy, the first place to look is in your mind. Ask yourself what you have been thinking and believing. For example, I have learned that when I am suspicious of people or believe bad things about them, it makes me sad. Sometimes it even makes me angry. But, when I believe the best, which is what love does (1 Corinthians 13:7), then I have joy. Joy can be anything from extreme hilarity to calm delight, and I love to live each day in the calm delight God offers us. This helps me enjoy life.

Of course, I also enjoy a belly laugh that lasts a long time. One day last week Dave was especially funny, and I laughed very hard on and off for at least two hours. Sometimes when I do that, I am not sure if the other person is funny or if I am desperate for laughter, but either way, I love to laugh. God has given us the ability to laugh, so He must want us to do it.

Proverbs 17:22 says, "A happy heart is good medicine and a cheerful mind works healing, but a broken spirit dries up the bones." An article on Help Guide.org says, "It's true: laughter is strong medicine. It draws people together in ways that trigger healthy physical and emotional changes in the body. Laughter strengthens your immune system, boosts mood, diminishes pain, and protects you from the damaging effects of stress."[14]

According to US Preventative Medicine, children laugh up to three hundred times each day, and the average adult laughs seventeen times per day.[15] Even seventeen seems like a lot for some people I know. This is just my opinion, but there are most likely some people who have not laughed seventeen times in a year, let alone in one day. If people are severely depressed, they probably never laugh, and according to Mental Health America, 21 million American adults are severely depressed.[16] Laughter is one of many things that can help alleviate depression,[17] so find something funny and laugh. Watch a funny movie, listen to a clean comedian, or spend time with a friend who has a great sense of humor. You can even laugh at yourself. We all do unique things that are funny.

Laughter can help alleviate depression.

Life has become very complex, and many people—including millions of teenagers—are confused and unhappy. More teenagers than ever are dying by suicide or contemplating it. Suicide is the second leading cause of death in the United States for people aged ten to thirty-four.[18] This is a shocking number. Experts say they cannot figure out why so many young people do not want to live, but this isn't difficult to understand when we consider some of the bizarre things going on in our nation these days. There is a movement to push God and His will out of everything, and the more that movement succeeds, the worse conditions get. It doesn't take a panel of experts to figure out why. As Christians, we need to take a strong stand and do all we can to keep God recognized in every aspect of life.

Nehemiah 8:10 says, "The joy of the Lord is your strength." Since the devil wants us to be weak, he works hard to steal our joy.

LEARNING TO ENJOY LIFE

My childhood was stolen through abuse, and the household in which I grew up was filled with fear, not enjoyment. When I learned through God's Word that He sent Jesus so we could enjoy our lives (John 10:10), I had to learn how to do it. Even though Jesus had paid for my sins, I still punished myself when I did wrong. Two of the ways I did this were feeling guilty and not letting myself enjoy anything.

Anytime I did start to enjoy something, the devil would make me feel guilty about it and remind me of some type of work I needed to do. For example, if Dave and I took our family on vacation, I felt guilty about the money we were spending. I can remember, when I was a child, getting into trouble for laughing because I was making too much noise. My dad was an unhappy, miserable man who didn't enjoy life, and he didn't want anyone else to enjoy life either.

At Joyce Meyer Ministries, we call our television program *Enjoying Everyday Life* because I had to learn how to enjoy life, and I think a lot of other people do also. When I say enjoy your life, I am not talking about just the special times in life, such as vacations, holidays, getting to go shopping, or your birthday. I am talking about ordinary, everyday life when nothing especially exciting is happening. Today I am going to a baby shower for one of my granddaughters, and I will enjoy that. But yesterday I worked on this book most of the day, and I enjoyed that also.

THE SECRET TO ENJOYING EVERYDAY LIFE

I believe the secret to enjoying everyday life is to enjoy the person you are. Don't compare yourself with other people. If you are assured that God loves you unconditionally and that He enjoys you, you can learn to enjoy yourself. You don't have to focus on your faults. You can leave them in God's hands, knowing He is always working with you toward positive change. Philippians 1:6 says, "He who began a good work in you will carry it on to completion until the day of Christ Jesus" (NIV).

Be assured that God loves you unconditionally.

We all have things we don't like about our personalities or the way we look, but they are just "things," and they can change. While we cooperate with God as He works in our lives, we can enjoy the person God created us to be.

Don't focus on your faults. Instead, focus on your good qualities—and you do have good qualities. You have more good qualities than bad ones, and what you focus on will become the biggest thing to you. Perhaps you simply need to change your focus to start enjoying your life.

I remember how miserable I was all the years I didn't like myself and often even hated myself, and I'm sure it made God sad. He loves us unconditionally, and the more we let Him love us and love Him in return, the more we will be changed into the image of Jesus Christ.

As we close this chapter, let me remind you of these words written by Solomon, the wisest man who ever lived:

So I commend the enjoyment of life, because there is nothing better for a person under the sun than to eat and drink and be glad. Then joy will accompany them in their toil all the days of the life God has given them under the sun.

Ecclesiastes 8:15 NIV

11

Let Your Light Shine

Let your light so shine before men, that they may see your good works, and glorify your Father which is in heaven.

Matthew 5:16 KJV

As believers, you and I have been given what the Bible calls the ministry of intercession and reconciliation (2 Corinthians 5:19; 1 Timothy 2:1). This means God calls us to pray for others and do what we can do to see them reconciled to God if they do not know Him. We are God's representatives on the earth, and the only way some people may see Jesus is to see Him working through His people, including you and me.

Second Corinthians 5:20 says, "So we are Christ's ambassadors, God making His appeal as it were through us. We [as Christ's personal representatives] beg you for His sake to lay hold of the divine favor [now offered you] and be reconciled to God." To me it is an awesome thing that we are Christ's personal representatives.

Jesus says we are salt and light. Salt makes people thirsty, and light dispels darkness.

You are the salt of the earth. But if the salt loses its saltiness, how can it be made salty again? It is no longer good for anything, except to be thrown out and trampled underfoot. You are the light of the world. A town built on a hill cannot be hidden. Neither do people light a lamp and put it under a bowl. Instead they put it on its stand, and it gives light to everyone in the house. In the same way, let your light shine before others, that they may see your good deeds and glorify your Father in heaven.

Matthew 5:13–16 NIV

It is God's will for us to live in such a way that our lives make people thirsty for what we have, and that those who live in darkness will see the light in us and be drawn to Christ, who lives in us. People in the world are desperate for love, and God's love has been poured into our hearts by the Holy Spirit (Romans 5:5). God has poured it in, and we should pour it out. To speak plainly, we have what people need.

It is God's will that those who live in darkness will see the light through you.

LET GOD'S GOODNESS FLOW
THROUGH YOU

When we give away what God has given us, He returns more to us so we may continue to have what we need to help others. If we hold on to what we have and refuse to let it flow out of us to others, it will stagnate and become like a pool of stinky water.

Most people who need Jesus do not go to church to find Him, but they do work with you, live in your neighborhood, go to school with you or your children, shop in the grocery store with you, and help you at the bank or drugstore. People who don't know Jesus as their Savior are everywhere, but so are God's people. All we need to do is turn the lights on; if they are already on, then turn them up brighter. The way we do this is by getting out into society and behaving as Jesus would behave. Be kind, loving, generous, forgiving, patient, friendly, encouraging, and helpful.

The way we treat people is very important to Jesus. It also says a great deal about what kind of person we are. Jesus asks Peter three times if he loves Him, and each time Peter says, "Yes, Lord, You know that I love You," and Jesus replies, "feed [or tend] My sheep" twice, and once He says, "Feed My lambs" (John 21:15–17). I think He may well have been saying "If you love me, then help my people."

One time I went to a restaurant to eat after a conference we hosted. There were about twelve of us in our group, and the server spilled an entire tray of drinks on Dave—coffee, soft drinks, water, and iced tea. She was nervous and crying because this was her first day of work in the restaurant. Dave helped her not get in trouble by telling the manager that the accident wasn't the server's fault, that the restaurant was so crowded she didn't have enough room to navigate around our large table.

The server got us new drinks, and when she came back to our table, she looked at me and said, "I'm so sorry. I was already nervous about my job, but I have been watching you on television, and that made me even more nervous." Silently, in my heart, I began thanking God that none of us had reacted impatiently or in an ungodly way to the spill, but instead we had behaved as Jesus would have in a similar situation.

I'd love to be able to say I have always acted in ways that represent Jesus well, but sadly, there have been times when I have not behaved as well as I did that time and have had to go back and apologize to people, admitting that I was rude.

I have learned over the years how much we harm our reputation as Christians by not behaving as we should in front of people who know we are Christians. The accusation we often hear of Christians being hypocrites is more than likely due to Christians behaving in ungodly ways while also going to church, having Christian bumper stickers on their cars, wearing crosses around their neck, and doing other things that declare "I am a Christian," yet not being good ambassadors for Christ.

This subject has become extremely important to me over the last several years. I know how desperate some people are to be loved, and I'll say it again: As believers, we have what they need. We simply need to be willing to be sensitive to their needs and let God work through us to help them. Some people are hurting so bad that simply telling them about Jesus will not penetrate their pain. We must show them Jesus, and every Christian can do this if we will. It does require self-control and a lot of help from the Holy Spirit, but if it is a priority for us, we can do it.

You must show people Jesus.

INTERCESSION

Intercession is the act of intervening for another person. Jesus is at the right hand of God always interceding for us (Romans 8:34). If He were not doing this work, there would be a gap between God and us that none of us could be holy enough to cross. But through prayer, Jesus stands in the gap, and through our faith in Him, we can approach Father God in His name.

By interceding for others, we are bringing them together with God. Prayer opens the door for God to work in the lives of people who may not know how to pray for themselves.

Here are several scriptures that instruct us to pray for others:

And pray in the Spirit on all occasions with all kinds of prayers and requests. With this in mind, be alert and always keep on praying for all the Lord's people.

Ephesians 6:18 NIV

For this reason we also, since the day we heard it, do not cease to pray for you, and to ask that you may be filled with the knowledge of His will in all wisdom and spiritual understanding.

Colossians 1:9 NKJV

But I say to you, love your enemies, bless those who curse you, do good to those who hate

you, and pray for those who spitefully use you
and persecute you.

Matthew 5:44 NKJV

First of all, then, I urge that supplications,
prayers, intercessions, and thanksgivings be
made for all people.

1 Timothy 2:1 ESV

Confess to one another therefore your faults
(your slips, your false steps, your offenses,
your sins) and pray [also] for one another, that
you may be healed and restored [to a spiritual
tone of mind and heart]. The earnest (heart-
felt, continued) prayer of a righteous man
makes tremendous power available [dynamic
in its working].

James 5:16

To some people, prayer feels like a daunting task,
but it is one of the simplest yet most powerful things
we can do. When someone comes to your heart or

you notice a need in their life, pray right away. Don't wait, because if you do, you may forget about it. You can pray silently or out loud. But prayer does not have to be verbal to be effective. You don't have to be on your knees with hands folded and eyes shut. You can pray anywhere, anytime about anything.

Paul often asked the various churches that He ministered to to pray for him that he would be bold and preach the gospel and that doors would open for him to do so.

I thank God for the people who pray for me. I doubt I could do what I am doing if I didn't have people praying for me. I know one woman to whom God has given the assignment to pray for me, and she has been faithful to do it for forty-two years. Our prayers strengthen one another.

We can also pray simple prayers of protection over one another. For example, our son is flying to our home today from Utah, and this morning I simply asked God to give him a safe and enjoyable flight. It only took a few seconds and may have protected him from plane delays, being seated next to someone who was annoying, or even a plane accident.

TWO WAYS TO LET YOUR LIGHT SHINE

There are many ways we can let our light shine, but there are two that I want to focus on as we approach the close of this book. Our world today is filled with negativity and hopelessness. We can combat this in at least two ways: Be positive and spread hope.

Be Positive

The first way I recommend that you be positive is to choose not to join in negative conversations. If possible, turn them in a positive direction. If people are being negative about conditions in the world, you might say something like, "True, the world is not in good condition, but God is on our side, and we can pray and be a good example to others." If you are talking to unbelievers, such a comment might not be received well, so you could say something like, "Let's hope and pray things will get better."

In Numbers 13, Moses sent twelve spies into the Promised Land to explore the area to see what the land, its people, and its natural resources were like

(vv. 17–20). Ten of the spies came back with a negative report, and only two gave a positive report. The ten said the fruit is wonderful, but there are giants in the land (vv. 27–28), "and we were in our own sight as grasshoppers, and so we were in their sight" (v. 33). But the two spies who were positive said, "Let us go up at once and possess it; we are well able to conquer it" (v. 30). The ten negative spies saw the giants, but the two positive spies saw what God could do.

As it turned out, Joshua and Caleb (the two spies with a positive attitude) were the only two people who entered the Promised Land of the original group that came out of Egypt (Numbers 14:38). The rest of them died in the wilderness. Only those born in the wilderness—plus Joshua and Caleb—entered and received God's promise. Negative people lose their opportunities in life, but positive people create opportunities.

Negative people lose their opportunities in life.

In addition to Joshua and Caleb, the Bible introduces us to some other positive role models. For example, Ruth had terrible circumstances, but she remained positive and faithful (Ruth 1:16–17), and she eventually married the wealthiest man in the country (Ruth 4:13) and is in the bloodline of Jesus (Ruth 4:17). Joseph was treated unjustly but remained positive. He went from being thrown into a pit by his brothers due to their jealousy of him (Genesis 37:23–24), being sold as a slave (Genesis 37:36), and put into prison for something he did not do (Genesis 39:20) to the palace as second to Pharaoh and in charge of everything in Egypt (Genesis 41:39–41).

Anyone can decide to be positive. I used to be extremely negative. I had grown up in a household with negative people, and my life was filled with negative and painful circumstances. Shortly after Dave and I married, he asked me why I was so negative. I said, "If you don't expect anything good to happen, then you aren't disappointed when it doesn't." I thought I was protecting myself from disappointment, but I was only making myself miserable and closing the door to positive possibilities.

Thankfully, God has changed me, and now it's hard for me to be around negative people. If I can change, anyone can change with God's help—if they want to.

Spread Hope

The second way to let your light shine is to be a person who spreads hope everywhere you go. David said, "I would have despaired had I not believed that I would see the goodness of the Lord in the land of the living" (Psalm 27:13 AMP). That's an attitude of hope.

Hope means to expect something good to happen to you at any moment. Hope has a positive attitude. The world is full of hopeless people, but you and I can spread hope.

Jeremiah 29:11 helps us understand God's will for our lives. It says, "For I know the plans I have for you, declares the Lord, plans for welfare and not for evil, to give you a future and a hope" (ESV). Romans 15:13 says that God is the "God of your hope."

Isaiah 40:31 says, "But those who hope in the Lord will renew their strength. They will soar on wings like eagles; they will run and not grow weary, they will walk and not be faint" (NIV). Some Bible translations replace the word *hope* with the word *wait*. If you study the meaning of the word *wait*, in the original language of this verse, it means to expect God to do something good.[19]

When we wait on God, we are not passive. We may not be taking physical action, but we are very active spiritually. We are full of hope and expectation that something good is about to happen, and we talk as if we believe this to be true.

The Psalms are filled with scriptures about hope. Here are four examples:

> For the needy shall not always be forgotten, and the hope of the poor shall not perish forever.
>
> Psalm 9:18 ESV

Behold, the eye of the Lord is on those who
fear Him, on those who hope in His mercy.

Psalm 33:18 NKJV

Let Your mercy, O Lord, be upon us, just as we
hope in You.

Psalm 33:22 NKJV

But I will hope continually, and will praise You
yet more and more.

Psalm 71:14 NKJV

One of my favorite scriptures about hope is
Hebrews 6:19: "[Now] we have this [hope] as a sure
and steadfast anchor of the soul [it cannot slip and
it cannot break down under whoever steps out upon
it—a hope] that reaches farther and enters into [the
very certainty of the Presence] within the veil."

When we have hope, we stay anchored in God.
Our soul (mind, will, emotions) doesn't rule us, and
we believe that no matter what we think, want, or
feel, we know by faith that God will not leave us

helpless. We live each day expecting something good to happen.

Let hope be the anchor of your soul.

Will you let hope be the anchor of your soul and spread hope everywhere you go? If so, you will be letting your light shine, and that is God's will for your life.

Conclusion

Finding God's will for your life is not difficult, and it need not frustrate you. Do what you know to do until God shows you something else to do. Approach life simply with a positive and hopeful attitude. Help as many people as you can, as often as you can. Be thankful, pray, rejoice, and don't worry— and I can guarantee you that if God wants you to do something other than what you are doing, He will let you know. Follow peace and be led and guided by the Holy Spirit. Believe you can hear from God, and don't be afraid of making mistakes.

You only have one life to live, and God wants you to enjoy it. Always keep Him first in all things and be peaceful.

So often people are looking for God's specific will for them while ignoring the things He has already told us are His will. I pray this book has helped you understand more about God's will for your life, and that your peace and joy will increase dramatically. I pray that everything you lay your hand to will prosper and succeed (Deuteronomy 28:8), and that you

will be conformed (molded) into the image of Jesus
Christ (Romans 8:29).

Love,

Joyce

Do you have a real relationship with Jesus?

God loves you! He created you to be a special, unique, one-of-a-kind individual, and He has a specific purpose and plan for your life. And through a personal relationship with your Creator—God—you can discover a way of life that will truly satisfy your soul.

No matter who you are, what you've done, or where you are in your life right now, God's love and grace are greater than your sin—your mistakes. Jesus willingly gave His life so you can receive forgiveness from God and have new life in Him. He's just waiting for you to invite Him to be your Savior and Lord.

If you are ready to commit your life to Jesus and follow Him, all you have to do is ask Him to forgive your sins and give you a fresh start in the life you are meant to live. Begin by praying this prayer...

Lord Jesus, thank You for giving Your life
for me and forgiving me of my sins so I can have
a personal relationship with You. I am sincerely
sorry for the mistakes I've made, and I know
I need You to help me live right.

Your Word says in Romans 10:9, "If you declare
with your mouth, 'Jesus is Lord,' and believe in
your heart that God raised him from the dead,
you will be saved" (NIV). I believe You are the Son
of God and confess You as my Savior and Lord.
Take me just as I am, and work in my heart,
making me the person You want me to be.
I want to live for You, Jesus, and I am so grateful
that You are giving me a fresh start in my
new life with You today.
I love You, Jesus!

It's so amazing to know that God loves us so much! He wants to have a deep, intimate relationship with us that grows every day as we spend time with Him in prayer and Bible study. And we want to encourage you in your new life in Christ.

Please visit joycemeyer.org/KnowJesus to request Joyce's book *A New Way of Living*, which is our gift to you. We also have other free resources online to help you make progress in pursuing everything God has for you.

Congratulations on your fresh start in your life in Christ! We hope to hear from you soon.

Source Notes

1   Susan Kronberg, "Happy People Are Healthier. These 10 Ways
     Show It's Far from Fiction." *Jersey's Best*, February 7, 2019,
     https://www.jerseysbest.com/health/happy-people-are-healthier
     -these-10-ways-show-its-far-from-fiction.

2   James Baldwin, *Fifty Famous People: A Book of Short Stories* (New
     York: American Book Company, 1912), 143.

3   Henry Blackaby, *Experiencing God* (Nashville: B&H, 2008,
     2021), 70.

4   Norbert Juma, "Michael Jordan Quotes about Winning in Life,"
     Everyday Power, August 6, 2023, https://everydaypower.com
     /michael-jordan-quotes.

5   Dallas Willard, *Hearing God: Developing a Conversational Relationship
     with God* (Downers Grove, IL: InterVarsity Press, 1999).

6   Brian Tracy, *The Psychology of Selling: How to Sell More, Easier, and
     Faster Than You Ever Thought* (Nashville, TN: Thomas Nelson,
     2004), 17.

7   "Theodore Roosevelt Quotes," Theodore Roosevelt Center at
     Dickinson University, https://www.theodorerooseveltcenter.org

/Learn-About-TR/TR-Quotes/In%20any%20moment%20of%20
decision%20%20the%20best%20thing%20you%20can%20do%20
is%20the%20right%20thing%20%20the%20nex.

8   W. E. Vine, *Vine's Expository Dictionary of New Testament Words*,
    S.v. "Doubt, Doubtful, Doubting," https://www.studylight.org
    /dictionaries/eng/ved/d/doubt-doubtful-doubting.html.

9   William Shakespeare, *Measure for Measure*, act 1, scene 4.

10 Jim Kwik, "How to Turn Knowledge into Action," *Kwik Brain*
    podcast, October 30, 2018, https://www.jimkwik.com/podcasts
    /kwik-brain-077-how-to-turn-knowledge-into-action.

11 Walt Whitman, "The Sleepers," in *Leaves of Grass* (Boston: James R.
    Osgood and Company, 1881–1882), 331.

12 Roy T. Bennett, *The Light in the Heart: Inspirational Thoughts for
    Living Your Best Life* (n.p.: Roy Bennett, 2016).

13 "What Is Peace in the Bible?" Words of Faith, Hope, and Love
    (website), July 28, 2019, https://www.wordsoffaithhopelove.com
    /what-is-peace-in-the-bible.

14 Lawrence Robinson, Melinda Smith, and Jeanne Segal, "Laughter Is
    the Best Medicine," HelpGuide.org, February 28, 2023, https:
    //www.helpguide.org/articles/mental-health/laughter-is-the-best
    -medicine.htm.

15 "Does a Laugh a Day Keep the Doctor Away?" US Preventative
    Medicine (website), March 31, 2017, https://www.uspm.com
    /does-a-laugh-per-day-keep-the-doctor-away.

16 "Depression," Mental Health America (website), https://www
    .mhanational.org/conditions/depression.

17 "Stress Management," Mayo Clinic, July 29, 2021, https://www
    .mayoclinic.org/healthy-lifestyle/stress-management/in-depth
    /stress-relief/art-20044456.

18   Sally C. Curtin, Matthew F. Garnett, and Farida B. Ahmad,
      "Provisional Numbers and Rates of Suicide by Month and
      Demographic Characteristics: United States, 2021," *Vital Statistics
      Rapid Release* 24, September 2022, https://www.cdc.gov/nchs/data
      /vsrr/vsrr024.pdf.

19   "6960a qavah," *NAS Exhaustive Concordance of the Bible with
      Hebrew-Aramaic and Greek Dictionaries* (La Habra, CA: Lockman
      Foundation, 1981, 1998), https://biblehub.com/hebrew/6960a.htm.

About the Author

Joyce Meyer is one of the world's leading practical Bible teachers and a New York Times bestselling author. Joyce's books have helped millions of people find hope and restoration through Jesus Christ. Joyce's program, Enjoying Everyday Life, is broadcast on television, radio, and online to millions worldwide in over one hundred languages.

Through Joyce Meyer Ministries, Joyce teaches internationally on a number of topics with a particular focus on how the Word of God applies to our everyday lives. Her candid communication style allows her to share openly and practically about her experiences so others can apply what she has learned to their lives.

Joyce has authored more than 140 books, which have been translated into more than 160 languages, and over 39 million of her books have been distributed worldwide. Bestsellers include *Power Thoughts*; *The Confident Woman*; *Look Great, Feel Great*; *Starting Your Day Right*; *Ending Your Day Right*; *Approval Addiction*; *How to Hear from God*; *Beauty for Ashes*; and *Battlefield of the Mind*.

Joyce's passion to help people who are hurting is foundational to the vision of Hand of Hope, the missions arm of Joyce Meyer Ministries. Each year Hand of Hope provides millions of meals for the hungry and malnourished, installs freshwater wells in poor and remote areas, provides critical relief after natural disasters, and offers free medical and dental care to thousands through their hospitals and clinics worldwide. Through Project GRL, women and children are rescued from human trafficking and provided safe places to receive an education, nutritious meals, and the love of God.

JOYCE MEYER MINISTRIES
U.S. & FOREIGN OFFICE ADDRESSES

Joyce Meyer Ministries
P.O. Box 655
Fenton, MO 63026
USA
(636) 349-0303

Joyce Meyer Ministries—Canada
P.O. Box 7700
Vancouver, BC V6B 4E2
Canada
(800) 868-1002

Joyce Meyer Ministries—Australia
Locked Bag 77
Mansfield Delivery Centre
Queensland 4122
Australia
(07) 3349 1200

Joyce Meyer Ministries—England
P.O. Box 1549
Windsor SL4 1GT
United Kingdom
01753 831102

Joyce Meyer Ministries—South Africa
P.O. Box 5
Cape Town 8000
South Africa
(27) 21-701-1056

Joyce Meyer Ministries—Francophonie
29 avenue Maurice Chevalier
77330 Ozoir la Ferriere
France

Joyce Meyer Ministries—Germany
Postfach 761001
22060 Hamburg
Germany
+49 (0)40 / 88 88 4 11 11

Joyce Meyer Ministries—Netherlands
Lorenzlaan 14
7002 HB Doetinchem
+31 657 555 9789

Joyce Meyer Ministries—Russia
P.O. Box 789
Moscow 101000
Russia
+7 (495) 727-14-68

Other Books by Joyce Meyer

100 Inspirational Quotes

100 Ways to Simplify Your Life

21 Ways to Finding Peace and Happiness

The Answer to Anxiety

Any Minute

Approval Addiction

The Approval Fix

Authentically, Uniquely You*

The Battle Belongs to the Lord

Battlefield of the Mind*

Battlefield of the Mind Bible

Battlefield of the Mind for Kids

Battlefield of the Mind for Teens

Battlefield of the Mind Devotional

Battlefield of the Mind New Testament

Be Anxious for Nothing*

Being the Person God Made You to Be

Beauty for Ashes

Blessed in the Mess

Change Your Words, Change Your Life

Colossians: A Biblical Study

The Confident Mom

The Confident Woman

You Can Begin Again

*Your Battles Belong to the Lord**

Joyce Meyer Spanish Titles

Auténtica y única
(Authentically, Uniquely You)

Belleza en lugar de cenizas
(Beauty for Ashes)

Buena salud, buena vida
(Good Health, Good Life)

Cambia tus palabras, cambia tu vida
(Change Your Words, Change Your Life)

El campo de batalla de la mente
(Battlefield of the Mind)

Cómo envejecer sin avejentarse
(How to Age without Getting Old)

Como formar buenos habitos y romper malos habitos
(Making Good Habits, Breaking Bad Habits)

La conexión de la mente
(The Mind Connection)

Dios no está enojado contigo
(God Is Not Mad at You)

La dosis de aprobación
(The Approval Fix)

Efesios: Comentario biblico
(Ephesians: Biblical Commentary)

Termina bien tu día
(Ending Your Day Right)

Tienes que atreverte
(I Dare You)

Usted puede comenzar de nuevo
(You Can Begin Again)

Viva amando su vida
(Living a Life You Love)

Viva valientemente
(Living Courageously)

Vive por encima de tus sentimientos
(Living beyond Your Feelings)

* Study Guide available for this title

Books by Dave Meyer

Life Lines